Living Well

DESPITE ADV

Inspiration for
**Finding Renewed Meaning
and Joy in Your Life**

HARRIET CABELLY

REBUILD LIFE NOW
NEW YORK

LIVING WELL DESPITE ADVERSITY
Inspiration for Finding Renewed Meaning and Joy in Your Life
By Harriet Cabelly

Harriet Cabelly, LCSW

West Hempstead,
New York
516-214-4778
harriet@rebuildlifenow.com
www.RebuildLifeNow.com

DEDICATION

To the memory of my mother, Evelyn Winkler.

ACKNOWLEDGMENTS

This book has been in the works for many years. It has been birthed from the miraculous survival and recovery of my daughter, Nava. The meat of the book comes from the amazingly gracious people who accepted my request for a blog interview. I thank each and every interviewee for sharing from the depths of their hearts their very personal and painful adversities they have faced in life. They are truly a testament to the human condition: that despite bad things happening, there is always hope for recovery and re-engagement with life. What's more, that life can be filled with renewed meaning and joy.

I am forever grateful for having enrolled in the Certificate in Wholebeing Positive Psychology program, as the teachings of Tal Ben-Shahar and Maria Sirois have greatly impacted both my professional and personal life.

The work of Dr. Viktor Frankl has been a foundational stone of my life from the first time I picked up his book, Man's Search for Meaning, at age 18. Only now has it all come together, with positive psychology, and informed my life. It all makes so much sense and is a guidepost for living well despite adversity.

I thank Lori Deschene, founder of Tiny Buddha, who was my first and foremost guide and teacher in getting my blog and interviews off the ground.

I thank Jackie Charley, my editor, who has been so patient with me as I procrastinated my way through getting this book project completed.

Marty Marsh, graphic designer and self-publishing expert, has been a fun find from the wonderful world of online networking. He has taken my project and brought it into the world.

I'm grateful for hubby, Alan, for his easy-going nature and benevolent acceptance of me and my pursuits. His support in this project has been unwavering.

What a true gift to have life-long friends, Eve, Miriam and Beth who have been there to provide honest feedback, support and enthusiasm; and often 'on demand'.

For my daughters — Esti, who from a long distance, has shown sincere happiness for my pursuit of this dream; Penina, who has been my proud, enthusiastic cheerleader; and Nava, my greatest teacher in how to live life well. My life has been made richer because of her — and yes — because of her challenges. G-d bestowed her with a beautiful nature, strength, optimism, resilience, love of life and adaptability to help her live her best life, despite...

This theme of people living well "despite..." has always been a passionate interest of mine. Nava's life has been a most definite impetus in coming back to what truly speaks to me and what I consider to be my life's theme, and work. This book is my way of paying forward the miraculous gift of her life.

CONTENTS

Rebuild Life Now

Join Harriet's email list to stay in touch, get
newsletters, blog posts and updates and read more
stories of living well despite adversity at:

www.rebuildlifenow.com/sign-up

CONNECT WITH HARRIET:

Harriet@RebuildLifeNow.com

www.rebuildlifenow.com
www.facebook.com/rebuildlifenow

516-214-4778

"Life is an occasion. Rise to it."

Introduction

Living well despite...

If I had to sum up the theme of my life these words might just be it. We all have the "despite"; despite our misfortunes, losses, problems, challenges, major disappointments and so on. Nobody gets by unscathed. But, can we live well despite our adversities? And, if so, how?

It's no big deal to live well when all is going well in our lives, but my keen interest has been in those who have a lot of pain and hardship to deal with, yet still manage to — dare I say — thrive. I am in awe of such people.

What does it mean then to live well? It means living with a sense of meaning and purpose, with an ability to experience joy and satisfaction. It means to embrace the positive and deal with the negative; to live aligned with one's values; to live with intention and be an active creator of our life, to put our best self forward so we can positively impact and be of service to others while we occupy a place on this earth. But, inherent in life is loss. And, therefore, so is the need to cope in healthy ways with our difficulties.

When adversity knocks us for a loop, living well means taking on the challenge and integrating it into our life. It's not about succumbing to the problems and becoming a victim, or deciding on some level that our life is over because of them. It's not about becoming bitter; it's about becoming better.

I still remember the scene at seventeen. A hot, steamy New York summer afternoon. My boyfriend and I sitting by the water in Flushing Meadow Park, with the Unisphere and New York State Pavilion from the 1960's World's Fair looming in the background. We were talking about his mother who had been through so much in her adult life. We were two amateur philosophers sleuthing around with our existential questions centering on how and why bad things happen to good people, and how, despite it all, his mother was able to live well. She'd had a son born with cerebral palsy who was killed in his early twenties in a car accident; she'd had one mastectomy, followed by a suicide attempt and subsequent hospitalization, and then years later a second mastectomy. It was at this point that I had the privilege of meeting her and getting to know and admire her. Her positive outlook amazed me. She had developed a sense of appreciation for what she had that I found truly incredible. She'd channeled her energies in various new directions and had a yearning to learn as much as possible. She took life on and, in her last few years, lived life to its fullest.

I mention this story because I pinpoint it as a defining point in time for my developing passion for understanding how to live well despite adversity. What became the prominent theme here with my boyfriend's mother was not so much all the loss and pain she suffered, but the wonderful way she was able to live out her last years. To develop such inner strength and positivity was something I greatly admired in her and became drawn to in others. I wanted to know how she could do it — how she could take the bad and turn it around to develop a positive direction for her life. That was truly growth.

Little did I know then that, years later, I would have to deal with these issues myself.

I entered a black hole upon finding out that my second child had neurological deficits and would have life-long disabilities. A bomb went off, and I was shattered. Despair sent me reeling into a tailspin of grief and I spent an entire year with a therapist venting and raging, "Why me?" I was full of anger and bitterness at such a blow to my expectation of how things were 'supposed' to be. Was this my punishment for moving out on my single mother when my then soon-to-be husband had had a huge fight with her? Or maybe it was because when I was around ten my cousin and I sang ditties, making fun of mental retardation? Guilt can grab us all by the collar and try to strangle us. I was looking for something to explain the 'why' of my situation, but I didn't find the answer in guilt. Guilt, in fact, would suck me in and destroy me, but through my intense grief work I was able to defeat its grip. Eventually I came to the slow but steady realization that there are no answers to the perennial question of 'why?' The 'whys' are the unanswerables. The answerables lie in the 'how' — how to go on living with a new reality. Dealing with the grief was my first step into the 'how'. There was a shift in my emotions. My resentment and bitterness started to lessen and I began to see and feel slight rays of sunlight. I began appreciating who my daughter, Nava, was — a smiley, good-natured baby who seemed very content.

I have now taken my life-long fascination with how people rise above their challenges and have become my own version of a field researcher by interviewing people who have been able to 'live well' beyond their adversities; those who have been able to transcend. Transcendence — to go beyond — is, in fact, a concept that fits with every interviewee. They have all gone beyond their challenges to live, grow and even thrive. Many have used their pain to help others by serving or creating something greater than themselves.

In recording these interviews I realized again how much words — both written and spoken — are powerful vehicles for growth and change. They uplift, inspire, motivate and give us tools to use in our own lives. When I started my blog, Rebuild Life Now, interviewing people who personify this theme seemed like a great way to gather stories which would highlight both challenges and ways to transcend them. I wanted it to be a source of inspiration, hope and education for others going through difficult circumstances, and so I set out to do monthly interviews. I came up with a series of questions to address this theme of coping and integrating challenges into one's life and how to then carry on, grow and create a life filled with renewed meaning and joy.

I have conducted three years' worth of monthly interviews — 36 to be exact — which now form the basis of this book. All the interviews follow a similar format in order to bring out specific critical factors. In collecting the material for this book I sought out people with a wide variety of challenges, and I am very pleased with the diversity of circumstances I've been able to include. I'm also proud that I had the chutzpah to ask some well-known people to share their stories with me, a novice interviewer, and they all said YES!

There are commonalities and themes which I have expanded upon at times, using both my own personal experiences and my expertise as a clinical social worker, and I hope you, my readers, will take away tools, ideas, and perspectives that you can adapt and try out in your lives. Some of the comments I make at the end of one chapter may be similar to those in another because they share a common theme. I have included them at each point that theme is addressed so that you can dip in to any interview as a stand-alone unit.

Each story is one of success since the people in them have all been able to not just live, but thrive. I offer them as inspiration and as a way for you to see and learn that you too can do it. We are not fixed human beings. We all have the capacity and potential to be more than we are, and to change — even in baby steps. Small change can yield big rewards. Carol Dweck, psychologist and researcher who developed the concept of growth versus fixed mindset, says that our abilities are not engraved in stone; we have the ability to improve and continuously grow with effort and learning. If we believe in this growth mindset we will take risks, do more things, and believe in possibilities. If, however, we remain in the fixed mindset, we limit ourselves to what we are and to the idea that we cannot be more or better than that.

There is much literature nowadays that states that resiliency, the ability to bounce back from adversity, is also something we can grow and develop. Research points to it being like a muscle that can be built and stretched so as to enable us to cope better and come back to ourselves after we've been knocked down by life's hardships. With our human capacity for growth and change we can succeed at digging deep, finding and pulling on our strengths to rise above our challenges. We can live on well despite our pain and suffering, despite adverse and severely challenging circumstances.

— *Harriet Cabelly*

Reference List

Dweck, Carol. 2006. *Mindset: The New Psychology of Success.* New York: Ballantine Books

*"The work is in the 'hows':
how to live life well
despite my loss
and permanent
life challenge."*

Harriet Cabelly

CHAPTER 1

Mom's New Lease on Life

Harriet Cabelly

 I've always been a ponderer, an analyzer, an existential questioner, a seeker, a learner, a fun-lover, a seizer. My mother used to call me the 'philosovka' (probably a made-up Jewish version of 'philosopher'). Since 2002, however, I've become much more intense and intentional in all of the above. These traits had always been there, but their levels skyrocketed with the miraculous survival and complete recovery of my middle daughter, Nava.

In July 2002, Nava walked out of her rehab hospital after a year-long medical crisis. She was the one-in-a-million statistic who developed a life-threatening infection from medication given to control a major ulcerative colitis flare-up. We were trying one last thing to avoid having her colon removed. Despite the frequent blood tests to monitor all her levels she developed, seemingly overnight, a cough and fever. Soon after being brought to the ER, she was intubated and we were told it would be a waiting game. It ended up being a three-month life or death vigil. She had developed ARDS (acute respiratory distress syndrome) and nocardia pneumonia (a critical condition AIDS patients sometimes get from a severely compromised immune system). She miraculously pulled through this acute period and went on to a rehab hospital to begin a nine-month stay for intense rehabilitation and treatment. She fought her way back to health, regaining all her bodily and motoric functions one baby step at a time.

I felt a strong need to honor her miraculous survival story, and so for the next few years I struggled with the 'what' and 'how' — what to do, and how to live differently having witnessed this most incredible miracle. I wanted to create something new and different having watched the awesome event of a life be returned from near-death and literally be rebuilt limb by limb, muscle by muscle, function by function.

There was no going back to life as it had been, although in practical ways, that's exactly what I did. Therein lay my immense angst and frustration. It didn't seem right to just pick up where I left off. As her mother, I had been through something huge and defining. There was a tugging force inside me screaming out to do something with this miracle, to honor it in some big way.

I had been a daily eye-witness to hook-ups of every conceivable life-saving machine rotating upside down and right-side up; to tubes coming out of every conceivable hole with fluid bags attached, listening to every beep and bleep, watching the ups and downs of numbers symbolizing a life down to its minutiae. Now, if that doesn't make me appreciate and savor life, recognize its fragility and the 'there but for the grace of God go I' mentality, and somehow translate that into an 'I better live life well while I can' attitude, then what do I have to show for the miraculous return of my daughter, completely intact as she had been before?

To date I haven't done that big 'something'. I haven't started that organization, or foundation, or created something out of nothing (as you'll see some of my interviewees have). However, what I do see is that I've been living with more fervor, passion and intention than before. I am actively engaged in the familiar, but more so — seeking out the new and unknown. You could say I've taken life on with an urgent vengeance, refusing to put things off until... My growth and change has come from within and so I have been intentionally carving out and living a richly engaged life, stepping up and into life's awe and beauty, and yes, even challenges — always looking for ways to enhance my life and the lives of others.

Stepping out of my comfort zone to take on new things has opened up avenues of wonderful opportunities such as:

Public speaking — something that has become a part of my work today. If you would've told me years ago I would be doing this, I would've said you were crazy. I took this great practice from my school social work job and it is now a big part of my work.

Clowning and laughter — a Patch Adams clowning trip to Sicily was a one-shot experience, but it has led to my facilitating laughter workshops and incorporating laughter exercises into my work. Laughter is the universal language and the greatest stress buster.

Foster-raising a service dog — what did I know about that? I'd never had a dog and was raised with the "Uh-oh, dog ahead, better cross the street" mentality. But my husband and I did it, with the detailed help of a thick book of instructions. Wanting to give Yael back many times throughout our 19 month stint, I stuck with it for the greater cause in mind (purpose kept me going here), and a gorgeous, sleek yellow Labrador Retriever passed all his tests and went to carry out his mission in servicing a boy with cerebral palsy. This was truly a valuable lesson in pushing through the stressful times towards a greater good — it ranks high up there on the ladder of meaningful experiences in my life.

Nava's medical crisis was actually a second major life challenge. The first was 33 years ago when Nava was diagnosed at nine months old with a rare neurological condition known as agenesis of the corpus callosum. This is where the white matter connecting the two hemispheres in the brain does not develop normally during pregnancy, and there is either a partial or complete absence of the corpus callosum. In Nava's case there is a partial absence of this connecting bundle of tissues. Being told that she would have life-long disabilities in some form sent me into a tailspin of grief.

I attended a lecture at a special education preschool given by a psychologist, Dr. Ken Moses, on the grieving process and the loss of the perfect child. His words touched every nerve in my body. I called him up the next day and set up an appointment that was to be the beginning of my year-long journey into, and through, the darkest time and the deepest hole in my being. After working through the torturous feelings of grief, the work focused on rebuilding new dreams and hopes more in line with what was, rather than what one expected, planned and hoped for. As Dr. Ken Moses said, when our dreams of the perfect child have been shattered, we must build and attach ourselves to new ones.

This speaks to all losses. We must readjust ourselves to the reality of what is, and go from there. It is an arduous process, and one that must be revisited time and again as life's milestones bring up both old and new feelings of grief. Each of these must, of course, be dealt with, but hopefully it gets easier once the initial work of readjustment has been done.

However, I struggled with the 'whys' but eventually came to accept the fact that there are no real answers to the questions:

Why my child?

Why do bad things happen to good people?

Why me?

I ended up recognizing that the work is in the 'hows':

How to live life well, despite my loss and permanent life challenge.

I became very focused on how I wanted to raise my daughter with special needs. I wanted her to be the best she could be, to maximize her potential, to be as independent as possible and to feel good about herself, knowing that emotional strength and self-esteem are what carry us through the thick and thin of life.

In addition, after finding tremendous relief from my pain as a result of a year of therapy and support, I decided I wanted to pursue a master's degree in social work and serve in this area of grief, loss and growth. I wanted to be of support and guidance to others on their painful journey. I took the turtle route for my master's degree, taking five years to complete it as a part-time student. I even had a third child along the way. But time goes by and things get done. I proudly donned my cap and gown, had my three little ones watch mommy graduate, and began working part-time for an agency, counseling high-risk families.

However, when my life took another turn and I ended my marriage, I totally went off my intended professional track and heeded my mother's advice. I got a job in the school system so I could be there for my children when they came home each day, and be off when they were off — during vacation breaks and summertime. Working in the public school system afforded this great schedule. School social work was not what I had in mind, however, when I initially thought about this field. But as I was getting divorced, I knew I couldn't exist on an agency salary. My mother had also been through this. As a divorced parent raising me, she worked in the local high school as the principal's secretary for my entire childhood and teen years, and had a work schedule that coincided with my schooling.

And so I remained in my school job for twenty years. It served a purpose by giving me the time and ability to do all the hands-on work with Nava after school — taking her to all her therapies and appointments and being the available and involved mom I wanted to be for my children. I always said my 'real' work began after three thirty, when I switched into 'mommyhood' gear. My school job was a means to an end. My last few years there did become better and more fulfilling as I took on new initiatives to develop myself professionally and create more interesting avenues. I began facilitating parent book clubs which opened up a world of personal growth and exploration for the parents as well as me. To this day I'm still leading them. In addition, I gave more presentations and workshops; something that definitely helped build my confidence and launch me into being what I am today — a speaker, facilitator, and presenter of workshops on topics such as parenting, resilience, grief and growth.

I have returned to my original intention of work — and the theme of my life — which has continued to expand with my own personal growth and further education into the rich and flourishing field of positive psychology, or in its most simplistic terms — living well. According to the founder of positive psychology, Martin Seligman, it is the "scientific study of optimal human functioning [that] aims to discover and promote the factors that allow individuals and communities to thrive." (Seligman) All of its correlates of resilience, purpose and meaning, joy, authenticity, values, character strengths, gratitude, attitude, post-traumatic growth, relationships, and service — among others — connect with me deeply in my personal life, my work, and what I have set forth here in this book.

Reference List

Seligman, Martin, *"What is positive psychology?"* http://posi tivepsychology.org.uk/what-is-positive-psychology/

CHAPTER 2

Grief in the Rugged Outdoors, Alone

"I accepted her death as my rebirth."

Cheryl Strayed is the author of the best seller, *Wild*, in which she writes of her journey through grief back to life after the tragic loss of her mother. And a {literal} journey it was as she hiked 1,100-miles along the Pacific Crest Trail (PCT) out west.

"It seemed like years ago now — as I stood barefoot on that mountain in California — in a different lifetime, really, when I'd make the arguably unreasonable decision to take a long walk alone on the PCT in order to save myself."

What personal qualities have helped you carry on and move in a positive direction?

One of the last things my mother said to me before she died was that I was a seeker. I didn't understand at the time how right she was, but now I do. My impulse to reach and dig and get to another emotional or psychological place, to understand a new thing, served me well when I had to rage against my mother's death at the age of 45. And later, when I had to heal my sorrow and learn how to live without her.

Did you go through a period of self-pity? If so, what helped lift you out?

One time, about two years after my mother died, I was with a group of women on Mother's Day. We'd rented a cabin for the

23

weekend and, since none of us were with our mothers, we went around in a circle taking turns saying something about our moms by way of honoring them. I was the only one with a dead mother. These women were kind to me, but I remember feeling an unreasonable amount of unexpressed resentment toward them. It felt so unfair that they got to have moms and I didn't. (And then of course I felt guilty for feeling that way.)

I let go of my self-pity over time, as I grew up and accepted the fact that I would never get my mother back. I also met many people who'd also lost their parents young, and they were a great consolation to me. I don't experience self-pity anymore, but that doesn't mean I don't notice what I've lost. I'm never with a friend, and his or her mother, that I am not aware of it. A little voice in my head always says, lucky you. But it's a loving voice, and one that understands complexity. There are many orphans whose parents are alive and well.

Was there a specific moment, thought, or epiphany that helped to bring you to a better place mentally/psychologically, or did it evolve?

I had many epiphanies that together formed an evolution. The hardest part about losing one's primary parent in one's teens or twenties is that you're still trying to form your identity, to figure out who you're going to be in the world, and smack dab in the midst of that, you've lost the person who'd defined you and against whom you'd defined yourself. You're grieving so hard, but you're also trying to grow up.

Those things are utterly tangled together for me. I don't know what was youthful angst and confusion and what was my grief, and I never will. I can't imagine what my life would have been like if my mother hadn't died. I've learned as much from her in her death as I did in her life. I had to stitch my own stories with the threads of her absence. At a certain point I became willing to do that. I accepted her death as my rebirth, whether I liked it or not. I was on a big journey when this really became clear to me — on an 1100-mile solo hike on the Pacific Crest Trail, which I wrote about in my memoir, Wild. The summer I hiked the trail was a time of many epiphanies. My experience on the PCT changed me forever. It was my evolution.

What are/were your day-to-day coping skills that keep you afloat?

I miss my mother every day, but my grief has lessened over time. It doesn't feel like the great weight that will sink me anymore. When it did feel that way in the four or five years after her death, I found comfort in my friendships, in silence and solitude, in the wilderness, and in my writing. Acceptance was probably the most important coping skill. I found solace in simply sitting with my sorrow. There's a lot of strength in crying the tears that need to be cried and letting go of what cannot any longer be held.

In general, how have you managed to rebuild your life after your losses?

By moving forward. By searching out love and goodness. By keeping faith with the things that brought me the most inner peace. By mothering my children with the same big love my mother mothered me. By becoming the woman my mother raised me to be, even though she didn't get to be here to see her.

What advice do you have for someone going through loss in the hope of coming out of the darkness intact?

There are dark days and painfully bright nights in this life. We have the capacity to survive them. We know this because so many others have, and are, and will. It's an ancient tale. Trust it.

Wild by Cheryl Strayed

ৰ

WE MUST ALL FIND SOME COMFORT during our time of pain. We must lick our wounds and give ourselves the chance to feel and heal, knowing that healing means more than that flippant phrase 'moving on'. We soften to the stinging pain and we hold the loss in our heart — the love, together with the sadness. The waves of tears continue to wash over us but their harsh thrashing and breaking yields to a calmer, lower tide.

When a loss hits our very core, we must go deep inside, peeling away the outer layers so as to restore our sense of self. For each person that may look different — usually not noticeable to the outside world. It's the going inward and sitting with the sorrow that eventually frees us up to turn outward again with some form of reintegration of the past loss with the new present.

Ms. Strayed helped herself by connecting with nature. There's actually a name for this — eco-therapy. We all like to vacation in those paradise-Garden-of-Eden-type environments. We innately know they bring us some peace of mind, a de-stressing; we feel it.

Eco-therapy has grown into a complementary form of treatment which encourages people suffering from all sorts of distress to get outside and be in nature. Breathing in fresh air, from behind the walls of our pain, is invigorating, freeing, and shifts us to a larger-than-ourselves perspective. In looking back over my time living up at the rehab hospital with Nava, my daily walks, even in the cold snowy days of winter, stand out for me as my life-line, my therapy. I literally had to get out of the hospital environs and feel something more — a life outside of sickness. It was during this year that I discovered hiking in the nearby beautiful trails of Harriman State Park and connected with the "Wednesday hikers" group. A few years ago, I also put in a small waterfall in my backyard as my restorative spot. I've always loved listening to the sound of waterfalls so I decided to bring a small semblance of one into my immediate surroundings.

Nature shows us the cycle of life through all its changes. And similarly we, as part of nature, go through our changes as life and death envelop us. Just as the trees grow new leaves after shedding the old, so we too can reawaken and re-grow ourselves, holding joy and pain together — our love and loss as one — trusting in the process of survival.

CHAPTER 3

Autism and Beyond

Autism, and *on the spectrum* are terms that we hear and see quite often today. There are many debatable reasons why autism is so prevalent and may even be on the rise, but my focus and expansion here is on coping, managing and living the best life possible with this diagnosis. As the mother of one boy so poignantly states in this first interview, "This is not about a label or a diagnosis. It's about both unfolding and preserving the mystery of his self." It behooves the parent to find, focus and expand on the child's strengths in order to maximize his best self.

As the second interviewee in this chapter, Temple Grandin, states "Stretch them, otherwise they won't advance. Build up on the area of strength." She has a form of autism herself and certainly knows what it is to utilize her strengths. She lives out her potential having been encouraged in her areas of interest and talent, which then grew into her life's work.

"He who has a why to live for can bear with almost any how."

Nietzsche

Embracing the Strengths of a Special Needs Child

"I don't want to get lost in one vision of what a valuable life is."

Priscilla Gilman is a writer and English professor. In her memoir, *The Anti-Romantic Child: A Memoir of Unexpected Joy*, she uniquely and beautifully weaves her love of poetry, most specifically Wordsworth, into her story of parenting a special-needs child with autism. This diagnosis runs along a continuum of severity, with the core issue being difficulty in the area of social skills.

This is the story of a mommy as she selflessly and poignantly unfolds, and completely tunes in to the mystery of her son, Benjamin.

What personal qualities have helped you carry on and move in a positive direction?

The most important quality I have is that I am a genuinely very positive person. I have an outlook of optimism and hope with Benj — not meaning I want him to be cured or fixed, because I don't think there's anything wrong with him. But from the start it was, 'What can I do to help his life be more fulfilling and to help him become more fully himself?' I always saw all the therapies and special support not as a race to fix or cure him, not as tools in an arsenal as if I were fighting a battle against autism,

29

but rather I said to myself, 'I want to get to know my son better. I want to understand him so I can love him better and be a better mother to him.' And so when we would do the therapy sessions, I would try to look at them as opportunities to learn more about him and to help him. Not to help him change, but to help him become more comfortable with things he loved to do. For instance, sound sensitivity — helping him overcome those things so he could enjoy music and go to concerts because he loves music. Not so he can become normal, whatever that is, but so these obstacles to his engagement with things he absolutely likes, would be removed.

I've always had this positive, optimistic approach to life since I was little, but not in a denying way. I was always the little kid who cheered everybody up when they were sad. I was known for that. In a way, I think I was the right parent for Benj because he has a lot of anxiety, and I'm gifted at helping people with anxiety — and, I guess, helping myself with anxiety.

Those positive qualities pre-existed Ben, but he helped me develop qualities that have helped me along the way with other challenges we've faced together. He has helped me put things in perspective so that I don't get ruffled by little things that might have bothered me before. He's made me much more patient; he's helped me to become much more open-minded and tolerant of all kinds of difference, whatever form that takes; and he's helped me with being in the moment and not worrying and obsessing about the future — looking at each day, each situation, and each challenge for what it is. Those are great gifts that he's given me.

Did you go through a period of self-pity? If so, what helped lift you out?

I say this in all honesty — I never did; I just didn't. I think that part of the reason is that I had lost my mother-in-law who I deeply loved. When I met her she had stage four breast cancer so we knew she was not going to be cured. We got married, and three weeks after our wedding we found out the cancer had spread to her brain. We took a year off from graduate school, and with my husband's brothers we took care of her at home with hospice support for a year. That was something that profoundly changed me before I had Benjamin.

People look around — they have a child with autism or somebody with cancer — and they say 'Why me?' I would always think 'Why not me?' There are so many people in this world suffering, there are so many people confronting huge challenges; I just never thought, "Why is this happening to me?'

The other thing is that I was instantly focused on not wasting time wallowing in self-pity. I think it's a very understandable reaction and I don't judge people who have it at all. But I didn't feel that way. I thought, 'This is my challenge, my thing.' There's never been anyone with a developmental disability, even a learning disability, in either of our families. So this is completely new territory for us. I was resolved to learn as much as I possibly could, and I was going to focus on this little child in front of me and not waste any time with 'what if's' or my needs.

You have such clarity about yourself, and your personal insights are so clear. How did you develop this?

That's part of the result of writing a memoir. If you want to write an honest memoir, you discover what's true as you're writing it. It's not like you know all the answers and sit down and write it. You figure it out. It also ties in to Benjy — just as I want to know him and I want to help him be as happy and fulfilled as he can be, I feel the same way about myself. It's very important to be able to look at ourselves and say, 'These are my strengths, these are my challenges, these are my weaknesses,' because everybody has challenges and weaknesses. The more honest I can be about my limitations as well as my strengths, the happier and more peaceful I can be.

Was there a specific moment or epiphany that helped to guide you to a better place mentally and psychologically, or did it evolve?

There wasn't really one specific thing. However I would say I didn't have a very long grieving period. I focused immediately on helping Benjamin. The moment that made things easier overall was about three years after Benjamin was first evaluated. When he was assessed in 2002, he was diagnosed with severe gross motor delays, moderate fine motor delays, a host of sensory sensitivities, a language disorder (not language delays — he actually tested super high on certain things and super low on others). He was not given an autism diagnosis. I think he would be today. Ten years ago there were different criteria.

For the first few years he was in a mainstream pre-school. It was hard, and we had to do a lot of work with the school. My ex-husband was very determined to get Ben into a mainstream elementary school. It was wrenching and painful at the time as we were applying to first grade, and we found out his issues were really profound. Accepting — completely accepting that Ben did not have a condition that he was going to grow out of, and he did not have a condition that could be cured or fixed, or that I wanted to be cured or fixed. Accepting that he had a life-long condition with a lot of wonderful strengths that came along with it as well as weaknesses, and not racing to get him to be normal but embracing who he was, that's the moment where I never felt the same level of stress or worry or anything negative again. That was two years after he was first evaluated. The third year was very roller coaster-like. I don't feel like I'm on a roller coaster anymore. If I am, it's a much easier one, like a baby roller coaster. I don't feel my stomach dropping out. I don't lie awake worrying about him; I don't cry in my pillow at night. He's in a special school — he's not mainstreamed. I'm not concerned with getting him mainstreamed; I'm concerned with him being in the best environment for him.

What are your day-to-day coping skills that keep you afloat?

Meditation is crucial for me. That's something I started doing in graduate school. Twenty minutes of meditation is like a two-hour nap. It helps me be more time-efficient. People say, 'Oh I don't have enough time in my day to meditate.' But when I meditate I find I get things done in half the time I would have.

The other thing is getting enough sleep. I need a lot of sleep. If I don't get it, I get sick. I will leave a social event early so I can get enough sleep.

What thoughts propel you forward?

Not thinking too far down the line. Not thinking about what's going to propel me forward but taking it one season, one school year at a time. And not making assumptions about what Benj is going to able to do and what he's not going to do, three years down the line.

I don't worry or obsess about his future. I try not to put too much stock in certain milestones like, 'Is he going to be able to live independently?' I don't know the answer to that. And frankly it doesn't really matter to me. If he can, wonderful; if he can't, it doesn't mean his life is less. If it's the right thing for him, the best thing, then that's what counts. I think Benj will go to college because he's very academically strong and he loves school and learning. For some kids on the spectrum, they're not going to go to college, and there's nothing wrong with that. I don't want to get lost in one vision of what a valuable life is.

What advice would you offer someone going through this — being a parent of a special needs child?

My advice would be to not compare your child to anybody else's child, or your parenting situation to others. Focus on your individual child. Look for their strengths because every child has them. Use their strengths to help with the challenges. One thing we did with Benj — we used his strength of reading to help him connect socially. We need to look for those gifts. We need to focus on their gifts rather than only on the negatives.

Take time for yourself. Don't let your life become 24/7 worrying and obsessing about the child, because that's really easy to do. I think I did do that for the first couple of years, which was not great for my marriage which would've broken up anyway. You can't have a good marriage if you're totally focused on the child's needs. You'll be a better parent if you take care of yourself. I know that's really hard. I'm learning as I get older that it's not self-indulgent to go in a room and meditate. Or to say I'm not going to the party even though my friend will be disappointed, because I need to get some sleep. We can bring more to our children if we have more energy and peacefulness; if we are more centered.

Also, knowing that it will get easier. I subtitled my book, A Story of Unexpected Joy. I deliberately used that word, 'unexpected'. I got the unexpected. I didn't get the kid I was anticipating; I didn't get the family life I was expecting. In fact I've learned to see the unexpected as something that brings blessings with it. There's some deep joy in allowing myself to be surprised by my experience. Everyday there's something weird and magical that happens with my children, if I look at it the right way. Joy is not the same thing as happiness. There's a quote by Anne Morrow Lindbergh: "For happiness one needs security, but joy can spring like a flower even from the cliffs of despair." It doesn't mean our life isn't very difficult and challenging, but there's still a deep sense of something joyful in parenting our children. And they help us. It sounds like a cliché but it's true — Benjamin has made me a much better person. He's been my greatest teacher.

> "Oh dearest, dearest boy! My heart
>
> For better lore would seldom yearn,
>
> Could I but teach the hundredth part
>
> Of what from thee I learn."
>
> *William Wordsworth, 'Anecdote for Fathers'*

Seek consolation, advice, and support not just in psychology and education but in great literature. Literature was my solace. Humanities and literature are not frivolous entertainment; they can help us in deep ways.

The Anti-Romantic Child: A Story of Unexpected Joy by Priscilla Gilman

෨

 ACCEPTANCE AND *UNFOLDING* ARE TWO CONCEPTS that speak loud and clear here. As parents our job is to embrace our children as they are. But what happens when this is in direct opposition to what we wanted, what we expected? We naturally have expectations and hopes for our children. When the reality of *what is* does not match with our hopes and dreams, conflict and angst can occur. Internally we experience our own negative feelings, and externally we may enter into an onslaught of conflict and sad disconnection with our child.

We need to broaden our perspective and, along with acknowledging the obvious weaknesses and deficits of our child, we must begin to hone in on attributes and strengths. Every person has them. We must find them and focus on them, since attention to, and reinforcement of, those qualities will produce more of what we want to develop. In turn, these strengths will help us face our challenges.

It's all too easy to see all that isn't, all that's missing, all the problems. The key is to see all that is. We can then embrace it and encourage its growth.

As parents, that's the challenge — to not drown in the devastation of our shattered dreams, of all that we had hoped for our children to be — but rather to take what we've been given and grow that flower, appreciating its evolving beauty and potential.

We are here to become the best version of ourselves. That entails unfolding and peeling back the layers of what is most visible to the eye so that we can get to the hidden strengths which lie within each one of us.

"You have two choices
in your life; you can
dissolve into the mainstream,
or you can be distinct.
To be distinct, you must be
different, to be different,
you must strive to be
what no one else but
you can be."

Alan Ashley-Pitt

Beyond A Label

"Stretch them, otherwise they won't advance."

Temple Grandin is a professor of animal science at Colorado State University. She has pursued her passions, interests and talents and has succeeded in actualizing her tremendous potential despite having (high-functioning) autism. She is also an author, inspirational speaker and advocate for autism. Dr. Grandin has been listed in the 2010 Time 100 list of the one hundred most influential people in the world.

What personal qualities have helped you carry on and move in a positive direction?

Well one thing is just to have really good motivation. People with autism tend to get fixated on things, and I took my fixation and turned it into a career. My fixations were things like cattle shoots, optical illusions, kites, and building things.

I had some very good mentors. As a teenager I had a great science teacher who got me motivated to become a scientist. Also, Ann, my aunt out at the ranch, and Jim, the contractor — these were really important people in helping me develop. And then, of course, there's my mother. If I hadn't had her, I would've probably ended up in an institution.

What I see with people who have problems who succeed, is that motivation is a really important thing. In my work at the university, I've had a number of students who received masters

37

and PhDs with me and I held the back door open for some promising students who didn't quite have good enough grades to go in the front door. The ones who make it have motivation.

Sometimes you have to push a little bit. You take someone with autism, you have to stretch them. No surprises; surprises scare. But you have to stretch them because if you don't, then there won't be any progress. I'm seeing too many kids who are very capable of doing a lot of things, yet they don't even know how to do laundry or shop or know how to shake hands.

Stretch them, otherwise they won't advance.

Another thing is build up on the area of strength. My ability in art was always encouraged. When I was a young kid, all I wanted to do was draw pictures of horse heads, and mother would encourage me: 'Why don't you do the whole horse?' You want to broaden it out. You've got to learn how to use your ability to do stuff that other people want. People are not interested in just having me talk about cattle shoots; they want me designing cattle shoots. You have to learn how to do tasks that other people would want and appreciate.

I'm a big believer in developing your area of strength. If you're good with art things, let's work on art. Some kids are good in math, others are good with words, and some are good with music. Let's expand on that. Whatever strength a kid has, work on building up that area. It doesn't matter what it is.

We want to work on building strengths. My strengths are visual thinking and art.

Did you go through a period of self-pity or any other specifically difficult period, and if so, what helped lift you out?

I had times that were really hard. In my twenties I had a horrible problem with panic attacks and anxiety that got worse. That finally had to be controlled with anti-depressant medication. There's a lot of controversy with anti-depressants. But where they really work is in controlling anxiety and panic attacks. Getting my PhD was really hard.

How do you see yourself?

People ask me if I could snap my fingers would I not want to be autistic. Well, I like the way I think. Autism is secondary for me. I look at myself as a professor, a designer first. I define myself by what I do. I don't think it's good when a 9-year-old boy walks up to me and all he wants to do is talk about autism. I'd rather him tell me about the fact that he likes medieval times, dinosaurs, geology or Disney characters. One of the things that concern me now is that I'm seeing too many kids on the autism spectrum where autism is becoming their main fixation. I don't think that's good.

Was there a specific moment or epiphany that helped to bring you to a better place mentally and psychologically or did it evolve?

People are always looking for that single magic turning point, and there really isn't one. It's a much more gradual learning. You learn more and more things every day.

Social skills are a big issue for people on the spectrum. What is your advice on how to help remediate in this area?

You have to learn social skills. One advantage of being raised in the fifties is social skills were just taught to all kids. You were taught to shake hands, you were taught table manners. You were taught to say 'please and thank-you'. That was normal upbringing then.

The thing about being autistic is you have to learn these skills like being in a play, where you're not going to learn them unless someone teaches them to you. That's the problem (nowadays it's not taught well), and I think it hurts some of the younger Asperger kids because they haven't been taught simple things like how to shake hands — how hard to squeeze, not too hard or soft, not too long.

The normal kids can kind of muddle through it, but the

Asperger/autistic kids have to be taught. Like if I didn't say thank you, my mother would say, 'You forgot to say...' She'd cue me. She'd give the instruction. And if I stuck out my tongue at the post office, she'd say, 'That's rude to do that'.

I'm seeing a lot of older high functioning people on the autism spectrum who have good jobs and have been employed all their life. Then I'm seeing 'junior' having a much more difficult time getting a job because he has to learn things like being on time. This was drilled into me as a child.

And you can't just tell people off. Sometimes you have to do stuff you don't really want to do.

Do you have any thoughts or mantras that propel you forward?

I had some things back in the seventies. I remember the plant superintendent said to me, 'You always have to keep persevering'. And a cattle buyer told me, 'Trouble was opportunity in work clothes.' When I was getting my master's degree I found this poster by Alan Ashley-Pitt on creativity. This has been on my wall since the early 70s.

On Creativity

"The person who follows the crowd will usually get no further than the crowd. The one who walks alone is likely to find himself in places no one has ever been before.

Creativity in living is not without its attendant difficulties, for peculiarity breeds contempt. And the unfortunate thing about being ahead of your time is that when people finally realize you were right, they'll say it was obvious all along.

You have two choices in your life; you can dissolve into the mainstream, or you can be distinct. To be distinct, you must be different, to be different, you must strive to be what no one else but you can be."   Alan Ashley-Pitt

What are your educational recommendations to best serve this population?

Well, I think it's really bad that many schools have taken out the hands-on classes: music, art, woodshop, home economics, cooking, sewing, and steel shop classes. These are the classes where a lot of these kids, who are different, whether they're dyslexic, ADHD, or autistic, can excel. And we've taken these classes out. It's terrible. I speak on this a lot. These hands-on classes teach problem-solving ability. They take these classes out because of the tests. We need to be working the math and reading into those classes. Take a cooking class for example — look at the measuring you have to do.

You take that Mythbuster show smashing cars together. You can take that whole show and turn it into a physics class and have the kids do all the math on it. They may even do better on those standard tests.

So we have to motivate, stretch and build upon strengths.

Temple Grandin: How the Girl Who Loved Cows Embraced Autism and Changed the World by Sy Montgomery

Movie: *Temple Grandin.* Directed by Mick Jackson. Austin, Texas: HBO

ક♠

HOW DO WE IDENTIFY OURSELVES?

By our disability and weakness?

If so, we are limiting ourselves to and binding ourselves up with a diagnosis. Self imposed limits are nothing short of self-imprisonment. We are way more than our label. We short-change ourselves when we define ourselves by it. After all, we are a whole person first and foremost. It's true that we may also have a special 'something' that requires more attention, but beyond that 'something' we have likes and dislikes, interests and talents.

You see, semantics is very powerful and has a tremendous impact on how the world sees us and responds. Is the person autistic, or is she 'someone with autism'? Because if she is 'someone with autism' it's clear that she also has other qualities as well, and this becomes a more encompassing and embracing way of expressing it. Patch Adams in his movie of the same name says, "You treat a disease, you win, you lose. You treat a person, I guarantee you you'll win, no matter what the outcome."

We must engage and connect with the whole person, and remember that behind a condition is a multi-faceted individual who has a core and essence that goes deeper than the external problem.

Temple Grandin clearly had wonderfully insightful and supportive people to encourage her, who noticed and highlighted her strengths. We could all use a few of those who can spot the good stuff in us and cultivate it so it grows. And we all need to be that kind of person to others; someone who fans the fire of potential. Then we'll get people who live their authentic and best lives in sync with their strengths, interests and passions.

Chapter 4

From Victim to Thriver

"Thankfulness always trumps self-pity."

How does someone go through life being constantly stared at? Candida Sullivan is a pro at managing and living her life in a manner that elevates her and others beyond her external deformities. She was born with a congenital birth defect known as amniotic band syndrome. This is caused by string-like bands in the amniotic sac entangling parts of the baby's body. In Candida's case her hands, arm and foot have been affected. Her hands appear like mittens with the fingers joined together. Because of misaligned joints and spine, everyday activities create a lot of pain and swelling.

She shows us how to go through life standing tall despite the gawking eyes. She lives with pride, strength and lots of de-personalization, showing us where real value lies.

What personal qualities have helped you carry on and move forward?

The human spirit is stronger than we realize. We can endure so much more than we believe. My desire to raise my children, help others and celebrate life keeps me going. Sometimes all I can do is put one foot in front of the other and take one step at a time. But I never lie down and accept defeat. Giving up is just not one of my options. My faith and thankfulness to be alive help me to always look for the bright side of every situation, and to keep

43

trying. I don't listen to the negativity of others, but rather the encouragement of my heart.

Did you go through a period of self-pity? If so, what helped lift you out?

Yes! It is so hard to realize that I will never be completely well. The days I can't walk or function without extreme pain are difficult. No one wants to live with a debilitating condition or be surrounded by limitations. But this is my life, and I refuse to allow anyone or anything to take it from me. Life is hard and it will always come with hardships, but I'm learning to embrace my challenges. No one gets to pick the easy option. We all have circumstances to overcome, and challenges that need embracing. Sometimes we just have to dig deep into the depths of our heart and will, and amaze ourselves. We are all capable of so much more than our minds can even comprehend.

Was there a specific moment or epiphany that helped guide you to a better place mentally and psychologically?

The realization that I could have died changed my life. I had spent many years crying over my scars, and neglected to be thankful for my life. When it occurred to me that God spared me, all of my views changed. I transformed from a victim into a survivor. My scars are not a punishment, but instead are a wonderful expression, exemplifying God's love and mercy for me. I believe God spared me for a reason and I want to spend my life telling of the hope and love inside of me.

What were/are your day-to-day coping skills that keep you afloat?

A positive attitude and faith are my saving grace. However we decide to look at any situation is exactly how it will be. I always search for the good in my life. I'm on a strict diet, exercise routine and assortment of vitamins just to keep going. And every morning I have my coffee with God. I pray, meditate and ask for strength and guidance for each day and trial. God may not always remove the storms from my life but He will show me how to overcome them. Thankfulness always trumps self-pity.

What thoughts propel you forward?

God spared me for a reason and I want to live my life for Him. My life should never be just about me, but more about my God and the plans He has for me. Since the release of my children's books, I have traveled the nation and made 49 school visits in nine different counties. It is my heart's desire to stop bullying, and encourage everyone to celebrate their differences and become more accepting of others. I may not be able to change the world, but I can certainly leave my handprints all over it.

How do you deal/cope with people's stares, with those awfully uncomfortable looks?

Learning to deal with staring has been one of the most difficult obstacles for me to overcome. Throughout my life I've had people stare at me, laugh and point at my scars, drop my change, and scream and insult me with their ignorant comments. For years I hid my scars and tried to avoid these uncomfortable situations. Now I don't allow their bad behavior to affect me. I have learned that words and actions can only hurt us if we allow them to. It is when we believe the ugly comments that they affect us. Stares and whispers no longer have any control over me. All a stranger might see are my scars, but it is up to me to show them my heart. If they are staring at me, that just means I have their undivided attention and should use that moment to reflect God. I smile and always try to show them the woman underneath the scars.

In general, how have you managed to rebuild your life?

Acceptance is very powerful! Once I fully accepted my scars, they no longer had any control over me. I don't whine and complain about my hardships, but I thank God for my blessings. Things may not always be the way I want them to be but I believe God always does what is best for me.

What advice can you offer someone going through a difficult situation, in the hope of coming out of the darkness intact and able to live well?

Nothing is ever as bad as it seems. God doesn't give us hardships to break us, but to show us how to survive the storms. We are someone's window to God. When others see me struggle to do simple things but still manage to do them, and even praise God during my suffering, it gives them hope for their own life.

When I was a little girl I prayed every night for God to heal my scarred hands. Now I know without a shadow of doubt, if given the choice, I would keep my scars and the hardships they bring. They have opened my eyes to the real meaning of life and thankfulness. I'm stronger, more compassionate and have a deeper understanding of love, kindness, grace, mercy and purpose. I know that every single day comes with challenges and obstacles, but I'm so grateful for each one. And I pray every day God will bless me to help someone in some way.

All I wanted for my life was to be unscarred, but God had a greater plan.

Underneath the Scars by Candida Sullivan

Despite Your Circumstances by Candida Sullivan

⁂

THE BELIEF THAT WE'VE BEEN PUT HERE for something larger and more encompassing than ourselves, can carry us through and over huge hurdles and challenges. It begins to expand our focus beyond ourselves. We know there is something far reaching out there to aim for. A faith in God or a higher power/force can keep us afloat and carry us beyond our difficulties.

One antidote to depression is to 'do' for others. At a time when we've turned inward, stepping outside ourselves is just what we seemingly 'can't' or don't want to do. But it is exactly in the giving of ourselves that we experience good feelings. It's in the doing for another that our own veil of pain can be lifted, as we connect with them in a meaningful and helpful way. When we are solely focused on our own problems we become cocoon-like, completely wrapped up in our own 'stuff'. We have to push through to break through.

Going to the beach and looking out to the horizon or staring up at the sky gives us a perspective of awe at the vastness of the world around us. We see we're but a speck on this earth; and yet, as all the seemingly tiny stars each sparkle and contribute to lighting up the sky in its darkness, each of us has the capacity to shine and light up our life even in darkness. We were chosen to be here and life calls upon us to create our haven and heaven on earth.

Gratitude and looking for the good helps the brain focus on what we have, on that rim of the donut covered with sprinkles and icing, rather than on the hole of emptiness in the middle. It is possible to cultivate this mind shift where we focus on what we have, rather than lament over what we lack. We can train ourselves to pay more attention to the beauty of the rose, while still being careful not to get pricked by its thorns. Often life is not easy, but by being aware that we have a choice we can shift our focus and pay more attention to the positive.

Those stares that Candida withstands can be killers. They can keep us locked in our own prisons in such a way that we will never want to be seen. This only further isolates us and makes us live in that small insulated world of pain and suffering. Getting beyond those stares must begin with a focus on ourselves from the inside. We have to know that there's more to us than meets the eye, that our truest, most authentic selves are not our externals. That's no easy feat since our society is very outwardly focused. It looks at how we're packaged. However, if we can transcend that — especially when we have difficulties that are impossible to ignore— we gift ourselves with a better life.

"When you are immune to the opinions and actions of others, you won't be the victim of needless suffering." (Ruiz 1997)

"It is only with the heart that one can see rightly; what is essential is invisible to the eye." (Saint Exupéry 1943)

Reference List

Ruiz, Don Miguel. 1997. *The Four Agreements: A Practical Guide to Personal Freedom (A Toltec Wisdom Book)*. California: Amber-Allen Publishing

Saint-Exupéry, Antoine de.1943.*TheLittle Prince.* Houghton Mifflin Harcourt

CHAPTER 5

Supporting a Friend Through Illness

"Empathy translated into action equals kindness."

 Getting a cancer diagnosis is a life-changer. Nothing short of terror sets in and takes over our whole being. The world as we know it spins to a sudden halt and we get paralzyed with trepidation — fear of dying, fear of treatments and overall fear of horrific sickness.

Survivor of cancer, and teacher of how to be the best possible support to others going through critical illness, Letty Cottin Pogrebin is an inspiration to all, both in how she has dealt with her adversity and how she has taken her challenge and gone on to help others. In her latest book, *How To Be a Friend To A Friend Who's Sick,* the subject of friendship and illness came to the forefront for her as she went through her own battle with breast cancer.

How can we support one another through crisis and difficulties — what do we say, how do we listen, how can we be there for each other? Here Letty shares some of the answers to these questions.

What personal qualities have helped you carry on and move forward?

I suppose my general optimism helped me move forward after my cancer diagnosis. My habit of denial also helped. I'm very good at repressing the negatives and concentrating on the positive elements of my life.

49

Did you go through a period of self-pity? If so, what helped lift you out?

I think everyone who gets a serious illness goes through some depression or self-pity — it's only natural. What helped me was to refocus on everything I have to be grateful for — my wonderful family, work that I love, a basically OK prognosis for recovery, and the beauty of the world around me. It may sound corny but that's what lifted me out of the doldrums.

Was there a specific moment or epiphany that helped to guide you to a better place mentally and psychologically, or did it evolve?

Shortly after I received my diagnosis I thought about all the women I know who have had breast cancer and who now lead healthy, vigorous and fully-functioning lives. That realization allowed me to reframe my situation as something I would eventually get through and put behind me, as these other friends had. In the book I describe the three women — close friends — who helped me when I was 'in my cave', and I'm quite specific about what they did and said that made me feel better, stronger, and more equipped to endure the ordeal that lay ahead.

What were/are your day-to-day coping skills that keep you afloat?

My most effective coping skill was what I call 'normalization.' As much as possible, I tried to keep doing what I've always done. I had a yearning to feel 'normal' no matter what I was going through. I didn't want to become 'cancer girl'. For me, that meant maintaining an active social life as soon as I was able, spending time with my husband, children and grandchildren, doing my writing, going out to dinner or to the movies or the theater, hiking and traveling. Not all sick people have the strength or capacity to continue with their usual activities but, as I emphasize in How To Be A Friend To A Friend Who's Sick, it's still the case that their friends can help to 'normalize' them by striking the right balance in their conversations — always showing care and concern but never letting it turn into pity or suffocation.

What advice can you offer someone going through a critical illness?

My primary goal in my new book is to encourage absolute honesty on the part of both patients and their friends and family. Patients should feel entitled to admit what they want and don't want from the people in their lives; what feels good and what doesn't; when they want company and when they would prefer to be alone. By the same token, friends should be able to say three things to the patient:

1. Tell me what's helpful and what's not.
2. Tell me when you want to be alone and when you want company.
3. Tell me what to bring and when to leave.

Relationships based on this kind of candor can be a great relief and enormous support to someone going through a critical illness because patients who've established an 'honesty is the best policy' commitment don't have to pretend to like what they don't like, talk about their illness when they want to talk about sports or gossip, or fake appreciation for actions or gifts they don't really want. In short, the new illness etiquette is based on simple truth-telling by both parties.

How to Be a Friend to a Friend Who's Sick by Letty Cottin Pogrebin

೫

WHEN WE'RE WITH SOMEONE WHO IS SICK, it needs to be about them, not us. We need to take our cues from them. It would be great to be as forthcoming and honest as Ms. Pogrebin recommends, as that's the best way to get our needs met. But not everyone is comfortable with that degree of openness. Nonetheless, asking what would be helpful, wanted or needed is preferable to merely assuming.

In my attempts to be a good supportive friend, I've come to a realization. It's not enough to say, *'I'm here for you',* or *'If you need anything, let me know what I can do.'* All that does is put the burden on the other person to figure out what they need. It's too generic — and chances are they probably wouldn't tell you anyway. Similarly, I found myself saying, *"I'm here whenever you want to talk."* Again, it put the onus on the patient to be proactive and reach out. When others are in a bad way, they usually don't have the energy to do anything but think, feel and dwell in their illness — certainly at the critical points. The supportive friend, therefore, needs to be specific in their questions and statements, such as:

When is the best time to come over and do the laundry?

What can I make you for dinner tomorrow night?

How wonderful to anticipate a need and proactively step in to fill it. When going through difficult times support is the number one ingredient for healing. We need to feel connected; how much more so when we're facing a challenge. Feeling isolated and alienated by our troubles only adds yet another layer of despair. It's true that some people need to have alone time during their ordeals; some are more introverted, more loners; some like to talk about their problem, others stay fairly closed; some like to delve in and jump right into the waves of despair, others like to deny or distract. These are all different coping styles. But everyone needs to feel that someone is there, caring and supporting.

Asking for what we want, however, can be hard. And accepting help can be even more difficult. But it is so necessary when we are in a critical phase of our lives.

There is a lot of research showing that social connection is instrumental in our overall health. In fact it's one of the key ingredients in longevity according to the Blue Zones — those areas in the world where people live the longest and healthiest lives. Three of the ingredients for longevity fall under the social category:

Belong — to a spiritual community.

Loved Ones First — we must make time for family first.

Right Tribe — we need to surround ourselves with people who are upbeat and who value healthy behaviors and habits.

Brené Brown, researcher on social connectedness, vulnerability, shame and courage, says:

"A deep sense of love and belonging is an irresistible need of all people. We are biologically, cognitively, physically, and spiritually wired to love, to be loved, and to belong. When those needs are not met, we don't function as we were meant to. We break. We fall apart. We numb. We ache. We hurt others. We get sick." (Brown 2010)

Are you surrounding yourself with people who enhance you, who support you? Are you there — really there — for your friend in times of need? Can you tolerate a loved one's pain and really listen? Can you take yourself out of the picture and have it be about them when they're suffering?

We are often uncomfortable with another's pain. We want to run in and fix it. But we can't. And so (although it's difficult), we simply need to be with them in their suffering and know that our presence and support, and yes, even our silence provides comfort.

Reference List:

Brown, Brené. 2010. *The Gifts of Imperfection — Let Go of Who You Think You're Supposed to Be and Embrace Who You Are.* Minnesota: Hazelden

*"In the middle of
difficulty
lies opportunity."*

Einstein

CHAPTER 6

Mania in Check

"Recovery is not about the light at the end of the tunnel, but realizing that there is light — even if it's a tiny bit seeping into the tunnel — and you've got to grasp it."

My close friend's nephew took his own life. A few days later, a person by the name of Andy Behrman contacted me with his own 'rebuilding' story. Synchronicity was at play. Here was a chance to promote more awareness and education on a silent killer — mental illness. So in memory of my friend's nephew, a college student with a heart of gold and a mind filled with demons, I conducted this interview with Andy, a man who also suffers from bipolar disorder.

Andy Behrman is a writer and mental health advocate. Through his speaking and writing he promotes awareness around the "shame" of mental illness, suicide prevention and overall good mental health practices. At the risk of sounding too 'pun-ish', his memoir, *Electroboy: A Memoir of Mania* is actually quite electrifying.

Please shed some light on the condition of bipolar disorder and what it feels like.

My initial response to this question is that for me, bipolar disorder made me feel like "King of the Hill", but I was always scared I would lose this feeling. It's a roller coaster ride of euphoric highs and desperate lows. I exhibited much more mania than depression. I felt invincible during my manias and I was extremely productive, outgoing and the life of the party. But at the same time I felt like I was walking a tight-rope without a net underneath me. I was involved in drugs and alcohol, was overspending, racking up huge credit card debt, and was sexually promiscuous. And I wasn't aware of any of the consequences of my mania, which is why I became involved in an art counterfeiting scheme which landed me in prison.

Although during my manias I felt very much in control, in retrospect I know that I was very much out of control. I was flying from New York to Paris to Tokyo and constantly on the move. I wasn't sleeping, I couldn't sit still and I was delusional. There were times when I really thought I could take over the world.

My depressions, which came very infrequently, were not the depressions typically associated with "the blues." Mine were violent and rage-filled periods which were very brief. For me, bipolar disorder relied quite a bit on my "racing thoughts" and me acting on them. There were days I would wake up, have no idea what my plan was for the day and simply act on one of these thoughts — i.e. fly to Paris, buy a new wardrobe, contemplate a run for Congress, think about new business ventures.

This is a serious illness which is finally in the limelight. When I was diagnosed, more than twenty years ago, nobody had heard too much about it. I had never heard the term "bipolar"; it was referred to as "manic depression". People were not yet out of the closet with this disorder and they were definitely not speaking about it in public. In fact when Electroboy was published, it was one of the first accounts of this illness, and definitely the first written by a male. People regarded me and my illness as my being "wild and crazy", when in fact I was out of control and scared to death.

Bipolar disorder destroys lives every day, and people with this condition take their lives at a high rate.

How can this be managed to enable someone to live a functional and good life?

Bipolar disorder can be reined in and managed in several ways, but it must always start with the proper diagnosis. It is extremely tough to diagnose and I was misdiagnosed eight times by eight different doctors. One reason for this is that I "presented" myself to these doctors when I was depressed (usually agitated or angry), so they didn't see the mania. And why would I want to see a psychiatrist or therapist when I was on top of the world? So I was just as much to blame, although many of the doctors never asked the right questions about my behavior when I wasn't depressed (I believed mania was my natural state).

After my diagnosis, it was critical to find the right medications, to stabilize them and to stay on them, as many patients have the tendency to go off them after their condition stabilizes. I tried more than 40 different medications in various combinations and was unsuccessful. I then opted for electroconvulsive therapy (ECT).

It's important to point out that many people don't like to be on medication because their "highs" are dulled, and they complain of being uncreative. But in general, if you're working with both a good psychiatrist and psychologist (and I stress the need for both), taking your medication, are aware of your sleep pattern and the absolute necessity to get good sleep at the right time, along with maintaining a healthy diet and exercise regimen, one can manage with this insidious illness.

What personal qualities have helped you carry on and move in a positive direction?

I suppose I'd have to say that I've been able to move forward and work my way through bipolar disorder and return to being productive because of my perseverance and drive. From the moment when I realized I was "stuck" in my mental illness and when I finally realized I wanted to get better, my ability to acknowledge both my illness and the challenges was helpful to me. I've also managed to maintain my sense of humor through-out my entire battle, and this has been critical to staying well. I just can't explain how important it's been having a sense of humor through some of the darkest hours of a cruel illness.

Was there a moment, epiphany or thought that helped bring you to a better place mentally/psychologically, or did it evolve?

I think after I had spent time in prison for my involvement in my art forgery case, was locked in my apartment under house arrest and underwent nineteen rounds of electroshock therapy, I realized I had seen the lowest point anybody could see, and I didn't want to be living on a monthly disability check and be confined to my apartment forever. For the first time it seemed limiting, which may sound like the wrong choice of a word, but I was caged inside because of my illness. When I realized that I wanted more — a career, a relationship and to explore the world again as a stable human being — I knew I had to strategize to take steps to get well.

What are/were your day-to-day coping skills that keep you afloat?

Back then I had basic coping skills which included medication regimen and seeing my two mental health professionals regu-larly. That was almost all I was capable of doing. As I started getting better, I realized I could add a coping skill to my program as I was ready. Some of these included things as basic as show-ering every day, eating three meals and snacks, exercising, focus-ing on a sleep schedule, keeping order in my life, making career plans and coming up with goals so that I could be financially independent again. Oddly, I rely on these same skills today.

What keeps you going and moving forward?

For starters, raising two daughters, five and seven, keeps me going and gives me a reason to keep going. At the same time, I don't want to discount the fact that I'm quite driven and want to create another work about mental illness more important than Electroboy, which will be helpful to people suffering with mental illness. At this time I'm not sure exactly what that is, but I know I haven't written my last book on the subject since I have much more to add to the discussion. And finally, just living life, whatever happens on a daily basis — spending time with family and friends, meeting new people, seeing new places and enjoying every day keeps me going.

In general, how have you managed to rebuild your life?

That's a great question because sometimes I'm shocked that I wasn't just another statistic and didn't end up dead. I've relied on maintaining discipline and structure, and worked closely with my psychiatrist and therapist, as well as doing so much work in group therapy. But I think in general, I've always had the philosophy that recovery (and I'm not a huge fan of the word because I don't think one ever truly recovers from mental illness but rather learns to manage it) is not about the light at the end of the tunnel, but realizing that there is light — even if it's just a tiny bit seeping into the tunnel — and you've got to grasp it.

What advice can you offer for someone struggling with mental illness?

For starters, realize you are not alone. Twenty percent of the population is struggling in some way. That's a huge number. And in addition to not feeling alone, there's no reason to be ashamed. If you had diabetes, there would be no shame — you'd just learn how to manage living with it. Next, find a good doctor with whom you can work. Finally, when you're ready, sharing your story both with friends and family can illicit something you never imagined — support.

Electroboy: A Memoir of Mania by Andy Behrman

❧

PEOPLE OFTEN COME INTO COUNSELING wanting to have their problems 'fixed'. And my response is always, "there is no fix". In general, we 'manage' our issues. We integrate our challenges into our lives and struggle with the often difficult and ongoing task of managing. Addicts are 'in recovery' forever. They are not 'recovered'. It is an enduring condition that must be handled on a daily basis — one day at a time, as the mantra states.

Does one ever recover from the loss of a child? Does one recover from the sudden death of a young spouse? It's more the case that with time we begin to incorporate the loss and rebuild our lives. We build new frontiers using pain and hurt as our compass. We eventually come to see that there is a tiny ray of light seeping in, and we try to grasp it. It's not about waiting until the end of the tunnel — we need some little hints of hope and light to hang onto along the way. It's about stepping tentatively through the darkness and adjusting one's eyes to the light that seeps into the cracks and crevices of our soul. Our eyes begin to blink hard, acclimating to the light of our new reality.

There's a lot of shame still associated with mental illness, and because of this many people suffer alone which causes further alienation. It must be brought out into the open as an illness requiring recognition, treatment and support just like any other condition.

CHAPTER 7

Life's Natural Transitions

"Letting go clears a space in which new life can begin to grow."

"When we lose anything we cherish — a way of life, a loved one, a dream, a belief, even the day-in-day-out presence of a child at home — a space that was filled in our lives and in our hearts is suddenly empty. Sorrow, then, is surely a natural human response. And yet how reluctant we are in this noisy, busy, get-over-it-and-move-on culture to give grief its due."

Katrina Kenison is author of the memoir, *Magical Journey: An Apprenticeship in Contentment.* Whereas my other interviews deal with specific challenges or adversity, this one speaks to adjusting and re-adjusting ourselves to the natural transitions of life, to those unavoidable and natural elements of change and loss. There are feelings of sadness and loss simply by virtue of having our precious moments fade away into memories, by not being able to hold onto those cherished times in our lives. The old saying, 'life goes on' is much more than a flippant concept to which we must acclimate ourselves. We yearn for what used to be. We mourn the passing of time. And we must be constantly re-calibrating ourselves to what is, dropping off what used to be into our bin of stored treasures, and moving into new and unknown terrain.

How do we reconcile and integrate life's natural ups and downs so that we can continue living in an engaged, meaningful and positive way? Katrina writes about meeting and engaging fully with these natural and constant parts of our lives that often tug at our hearts and souls.

What personal qualities have helped you carry on and move forward?

Perhaps the personal quality that I'm most grateful for is curiosity. Curiosity moves me forward, as there is always something new to notice and wonder about — whether I'm taking a walk in the woods or browsing in a book store or having a conversation with a family member or someone I've just met. And perhaps the quality that goes hand-in-hand with curiosity is openness. If we are open to what life has to offer us, we tend to notice opportunities, small blessings, beauty and the simple pleasures of ordinary life. A gift cannot be placed into a closed fist, and not much can enter a closed heart or a mind that's turned in upon itself. So I try to cultivate these qualities, reminding myself to focus outward, to welcome each new day and whatever it has in store for me.

That is not to say I don't feel loss — no one gets to mid-life without being touched by grief, disappointment, illness, endings. And it's important to give those feelings their due, to allow time and space for mourning what's over. I do think that fully acknowledging and feeling our feelings is an important part of the process of moving on. But often those feelings are so uncomfortable that we try to stuff them down, to fill our bodies and our souls with food or distractions or medications, rather than honoring our very real need to grieve. Grief, fully felt, then begins to transform into something else — gratitude for all that is still good, still here, still worthy of our love and attention. It is said that grief and gratitude go hand-in-hand. Certainly learning to accommodate both is a universal spiritual challenge. I love that line from Dr. Seuss: "Don't cry because it's over, smile because it happened."

Was there a specific moment or epiphany that helped guide you

to a new place mentally and psychologically, or was it (and continues to be) an evolving process?

It is an evolving process, for sure. I don't think anyone ever gets "life" nailed down and figured out once and for all; we are always learning how to negotiate its challenges with more skill and grace. But there was a moment that stopped me in my tracks and made me realize that what I have to offer the world is enough. It happened during a month I spent away from home, doing a yoga teacher training. One night, in a special ceremony, our teacher was moving around the circle of students, handing each of us a string of mala beads (beads used for meditation practice). As he placed my beads into my palm, he looked into my eyes with such pure loving acceptance and acknowledgement that my own eyes immediately filled with tears. It is a powerful experience, to be seen and loved in that way. And in that moment I realized that perhaps I could make that kind of love my own offering in the world as well. It was definitely an "ah-ha" moment because it made me see that life didn't have to be as complicated as I made it out to be; that in any given moment, or whenever I felt confused or unsure, I could just choose the loving gesture, the loving word, the loving path.

This is hard to explain in just a few words, but I will say, learning to pause and ask myself the question, "What is the loving thing to do here?" has given me a new assurance. It helps me to see when I'm reacting out of fear, and to choose love instead. It has made me at once more courageous and softer, more confident and less attached to being right. I don't have to be right; it is enough to be loving.

What were/are your day-to-day coping skills that keep you afloat?

Being in nature and doing my yoga practice. I came late to yoga, and I've never been athletic at all. When I began, I couldn't even bend over or do a single pose. But I realized right away that if I was going to age healthfully, it was time to learn how to really live in my body — a whole new concept for me, who had spent an entire childhood avoiding gym class.

There is so much about growing older that we can't avoid — wrinkles, thinning hair, age spots, eyeglasses... But we can certainly take care of our bodies. Yoga keeps the aches and pains away. It keeps me in close touch with my physical body, and instead of getting progressively weaker and less flexible I am stronger now than I was at thirty. But there are emotional and spiritual benefits as well — I come to my yoga mat to learn to work with things as they are: the body I have today, the emotions I'm feeling, the sore throat or the tender knee, the thirty minutes I have between appointments. It's not about making things perfect; it's about being fully present to what is. And of course learning to be present and non-judgmental on a yoga mat is very good practice for being present and non-judgmental as we meet the challenges of normal, everyday life.

I also make a point of going out for a walk just about every day. Often my husband and I will go out right at dawn, a forty-five minute loop that gives us time to talk and reconnect with each other. It's the same loop, day after day, but even that routine has become something to cherish. We note where the sun comes up in the sky, watch the seasons change, enjoy our dog's happiness at being out with us. It's a wonderful way to begin the day — a little outdoor playtime before breakfast. And my favorite way of socializing with a friend is to take a walk — there's something about being together side-by-side and moving through the world by foot that releases us, and that makes wonderful open-hearted conversation.

What thoughts propel you forward?

Having watched a beloved friend take her last breath, I am more aware than ever before of just how precious life is, and how fleeting. For now, my family and friends are well, and I am in good health, but I don't take any of this for granted. And so what propels me forward is really my own awareness that it's up to me to make my own life matter, while I still can. Meaning is where we find it, and in how we choose to spend our days. I'm not talking about grand things here, but about the small things we tend to overlook in our constant rush to do more or have more or accomplish more.

I want to make sure my loved ones know how much I love them, and I want to acknowledge the great gift that is this life. Perhaps it is also this quiet sense of duty that propels me forward; having been given life, it is my challenge to recognize and appreciate its beauty. And I can do that simply by choosing the attitude I bring to even the smallest tasks. I can look at a pile of laundry to fold as an intrusion on my day, something to resent; or I can be grateful that my life at this moment is still so simple and ordinary. I can see the blessings in that pile of laundry. We don't always appreciate just how wonderful it is to be able to walk into our own kitchens and make dinner, until the day arrives when we can't do that anymore.

In general, how have you managed to recreate your life through this transitional course?

Although my book is called Magical Journey, there is a bit of irony in that title. I didn't really go anywhere much at all. Writing a book requires one to sit very still for a very long time. But of course, not all journeys require airplane tickets and extra shoes. Sometimes the most significant journeys we can take are the ones that lead us inward, to discover something new within ourselves. I began writing without answers to any of my "what now?" questions. I had no idea "what now." All I knew was that much I had cherished was over — my time as a mother with children at home, my friend's life, my youth, my editing career, even a certain stage of my marriage, which, after twenty-five years was in need of new energy and attention. But what I found in the process of writing was that I was slowly learning to let go of what was, even without knowing what might yet be.

And letting go cleared a space in which new life could begin to grow. Having finished the hard work of writing, I stepped out of that room and began to say "yes" to whatever life offered up: new friendships, invitations to speak, new relationships with my young adult sons, a trip with my husband that was just for the two of us. I realized that I don't have to get everything figured out, that the path is simply the one that appears at my feet, and I can trust it to lead me where I'm meant to go.

What advice can you offer those going through life transitions and changes?

Assess everything. Take a look at your old dreams; if they don't still make your heart soar, let them go and clear space for new dreams. Let go of old, out-worn ideas about the way things "ought" to be, and take a good hard look at things as they are. Change what you can change, and learn to accept and work with what can't be changed. There is a relief in surrender, a beauty in acknowledging that our white-knuckled grip on life isn't serving us or anyone else. Opening to change, welcoming it rather than resisting it, is part of the dance of life. Whenever the choice is between dancing and sitting it out, dance. When the choice is between love and fear, choose love. The rest will take care of itself.

Magical Journey: An Apprenticeship in Contentment by Katrina Kenison

❧

THE NATURE OF LIFE IS IMPERMANENT and we are called upon to be in constant movement with the changing of the tide; moving with the ebb and flow of life's transitions. Some changes call for much more difficult adjustments — those heart-wrenching crises such as debilitating illness and disability, or the loss of loved ones that brings us to our knees.

However, loss encompasses more than just the awful situations that cause us so much pain. The necessary, predictable and natural courses of life give way to loss as well. For the baby who's weaning, losing the breast and moving on to the cup is not easy. It might be sad for the parent too. But we know that moving on to the cup is best for the baby's growth. During toilet training too, where he's losing the security of the diaper and moving on to the toilet, it can be traumatic watching that poop be flushed away. Both phases involve a letting go of something in order to move on to the next stage.

Moving away from the familiar, comfortable and predictable world to unfamiliar territory is uncomfortable and even a bit scary. We are all creatures of habit and we like to stay put. But life isn't set up like that. We are not static or stationary. As animate beings, we are made to move and grow, otherwise we'd regress and lose our abilities; our muscles would weaken and atrophy. We'd lose our vim and vigor.

We need the ability, both in attitude and behaviors, to handle change. Oftentimes we're simply sad to leave the old and move on to the new. Dr. Seuss's line that Ms. Kenison mentioned, "Don't cry because it's over, smile because it happened", is a wonderful way to view transitions and life's natural changes. We can hold them both together. We can cry because the good time is over, but the key is to smile and appreciate that it happened. Tears and joy can stand side by side.

The Seals and Crofts' title song, *We May Never Pass This Way Again,* often reminds me to be present in the joy of the moment. I know something wonderful will end and I want to revel in its current happening. At my daughter's wedding I told her (as well as myself) to take it in and be aware of every moment as it was happening because it would all be just a memory in six hours' time. The wedding we plan for, the vacation we can't wait for, the infancy period of a child's life — be in them all as they are happening. Because "we may never pass this way again." This is a way of enhancing and enriching our lives — to really feel, focus and appreciate the moments as they occur. As Katrina writes, "Having been given life, it is my challenge to recognize and appreciate its beauty."

What are we doing with the gift of life? Are we noticing, appreciating and frolicking in its wonder and awesomeness? Can we see some rays of sunlight peeking in even through the cloud of hardship? Herein lies our challenge: to be able to rise up above our difficulties and still be able to recognize and appreciate the beauty of life; maybe not in that moment but eventually.

"There is a relief in surrender, a beauty in acknowledging that our white-knuckled grip on life isn't serving us or anyone else."

Sometimes we hold on so tight to what we want even though a new reality dictates something different. It's hard to let go of our expectations and 'shoulds'. We hold on for dear life while everything around us is changing. In the movie, The Artist, the main character has tremendous difficulty moving from acting in silent movies to the new reality of sound movies, even to the point where he almost takes his own life. His girlfriend, however, quickly adjusts and becomes very successful at dancing in the new genre, while he's falling into a pit of despair. Loosening our grasp on what was and opening to what is widens our scope of vision and possibilities.

CHAPTER 8

The Murder of a Child

Losing a child is one of the worst losses a person can experience. And losing a child in an unthinkably horrific and evil manner is incomprehensible.

These next two interviewees have each lost sons in a most brutal way motivated by hatred. Miraculously they have been able to push through and beyond with a newly discovered sense of purpose — one that emerged out of their pain. They each went on to create an organization to educate and help bring relief to the bereaved.

*"Although the world
is full of suffering,
it is full also
of the overcoming
of it."*

Helen Keller

Preserving a Legacy With a Cause

"I focus on things I can change."

"We are trying to do what we think Matt would want us to do with this opportunity of having a voice. He's with me every day when I do this. I know it or I couldn't do this because I'm a shy, private person."

Judy Shepard is the founder and director of the Matthew Shepard Foundation. In the fall of 1998 the names Matthew Shepard and Laramie, Wyoming became unfortunate household names across the country as people watched and listened intently to updates on Matthew's medical status. He was a victim of a horrific anti-gay, hate crime which took his life.

Ms. Shepard and her husband took their loss and turned it into a cause: to make our world a more tolerant, compassionate and respectful one. Thus the Matthew Shepard Foundation was set up to carry on Matthew's legacy and promote his causes of social justice and equality for all.

We need all the consciousness-raising and education we can get around these issues of bullying, taunting and violent hate crimes. It's not about whether we agree or not with someone's lifestyle or choices; it's about safety for all.

What personal qualities have helped you carry on and move in a positive direction?

71

I don't think I can answer that question about myself — too introspective — but I'll try. I tend to go with what feels right and not question myself about why. I trust my instincts about people and situations.

Did you go through a period of self-pity? If so, what helped lift you out?

I have never been one to spend time on things that can't be changed, so "self-pity" is a foreign concept to me. I'd rather move forward with "lessons learned."

Was there a specific moment, thought, or epiphany that helped guide you to a better place mentally, or has it slowly evolved?

With this question, you are assuming that I was once in a bad place or a worse place than I am now. Of course things have evolved because of my life experiences since Matt's death, but I'm not sure I would say my mental state is "better." I grieved, I cried and I still do, but I have figured out a way which works for me to keep Matt and his dreams alive. I have an opportunity to be a game changer in my own way.

What are your day-to-day coping skills that keep you afloat?

Day-to-day coping skills — one foot in the present and the other in the future. I don't dwell on things I can't change but I don't avoid thoughts of Matt. I embrace them and go with whatever feelings come with those memories. I focus on things I can change. I embrace the family I have now — a family that has grown.

What thoughts/actions propel you forward?

My goal, and that of the Foundation, is to make the world a more accepting place for everyone, regardless of perceived differences. I can't bring Matt back no matter what I do, but I can preserve his legacy with my actions. I can continue to share my story so folks can see the growth of the movement for LGBT

(Lesbian, Gay, Bisexual, Transgender) equality — so they can see what went wrong and what we all can do to make it better.

In general, how have you managed to rebuild/recreate your life after this horrific tragedy?

I've had the love and support of countless friends and allies, and I have a purpose. I have a goal in mind, as well as an understanding that achieving that goal is part of my future, but not my entire future.

What advice, if any, would you offer someone going through a tragedy, in the hope of coming through the darkness intact?

I think you are assuming that one can emerge from the darkness, that it is a possibility. In my personal experience, as well as that of many very close friends and family members, you don't "emerge." The darkness is always there; it just gets different. It becomes something you can look at with some objectivity. We still have joy and happiness in our lives; it's just different. At least, that is what it has been for my family to date.

My advice is not to let anyone tell you the accepted time limit for grief — it is limitless. That being said, it must also become something you embrace rather than fear. We've encouraged our friends and family to still share memories of Matt, not to shy away from remembering him. He will always be a part of our lives and that is a good thing.

The Meaning of Matthew by Judy Shepard

The Matthew Shepard Story (film). Directed by Roger Spottiswoode, 2002.

The Laramie Project (documentary). Directed by Moisés Kaufman, 2002.

ک

GRIEF HAS NO CALENDAR. In our society, people have a hard time with painful feelings. They want to know that we've moved on, that we're OK now, and that it's time enough to be better. We're a quick-fix culture and don't like feeling too much for too long. We take pills to numb the pain. We indulge in alcohol. We are great at avoidance, and being overly busy keeps us distracted and out of touch with our pain. Sometimes, of course, we need to distract ourselves so we can function and find some reprieve, but to do this habitually and inhibit our feelings just pushes them inward where they fester, only to rear their heads again later on. Sometimes they get camouflaged by acting-out behaviors and ultimately give way to a worse condition. It's like a tube of toothpaste that oozes out from all the little holes of wear and tear and ends up creating a bigger mess.

We must allow ourselves to feel and go into the grime of our grief in order to come through it intact.

As Shakespeare so poignantly said:

> "Give sorrow words; the grief that does not speak knits up the o-er wrought heart and bids it break." (Macbeth, Act IV, Scene III)

It is precisely in allowing ourselves to feel our excruciating emotions and to express them that we facilitate the healing process.

Purpose is also a big factor in being able to cope and live beyond adversity. "He who has a why to live can bear almost any how." (Friedrich Nietzsche) We all need something to wake up for; how much more so when we are stricken to the core by agony and experience a hole so big it threatens to encapsulate our entire being. At first we may need to stay with the covers pulled over our heads, cocooned in our blanket of pain. But eventually — and this is according to each person's calendar of grief — we need something to help us begin to push back the covers. We can then, however tentatively, put one foot down and feel the ground support us. To have something, or to create something that we care for enough to get us moving — however slowly — is a saving grace.

What got me pulling off my covers and getting out of bed each and every day of those nine long months living at the rehab hospital was knowing my place and purpose was by my daughter's side, cheering her on through every step of her fight for recovery. From vomiting her way to an upright position, to laughing through the excessive amount of re-watching *Mrs. Doubtfire*, I was there to encourage her through her struggles and successes.

At some point I thought of returning to work part-time (2-3 days per week). After going up and down trying to make a decision, it became clear to me that my 'job' was there with her. To travel up and back to my school job and then watch the clock, waiting for punch-out time when I could race back up to her, did not make sense nor did it seem worthwhile. Remaining full-time at the rehab hospital with her felt right. Driven by a clear purpose, I felt renewed in my strength and ability to cope and manage my 12-hour-days of being by her side. (I did take short breaks to do my walking and some mindless TJ Maxx browsing.)

Developing a new purpose after a tragedy can set our lives on a new trajectory. We are propelled forward by a new dream and we begin to re-enter and rebuild our life, albeit in a new form. Judy Shepard did just this. And she turned her pain into purpose.

What gets you up in the morning when sadness and pain holds you in its grasp and wants to keep you down?

"A hero in an ordinary individual who finds the strength to persevere and endure in spite of overwhelming obstacles."

Christopher Reeve

The Rebirth of a Mother

"Give from the pain."

"*Each day I have to work to go on; each day I decide to live. I am not the same person I was. That is the way it should be. Losing Koby means that part of me was killed. But rather than mourn the person I was, I work to bless the person I have become.*"

Sherri Mandell, together with her husband, founded the Koby Mandell Foundation as an outcry and outgrowth of their son Koby's murder in May of 2001.

Koby was thirteen when he and his friend, Yosef Ishran, were hiking near their home in the town of Tekoa in the West Bank of Israel. The boys were eventually found in a cave stoned to death at the time of the first Intifada.

The foundation helps bereaved parents and children who have tragically lost loved ones "rebuild their lives and create meaning out of suffering."

Mrs. Mandell is a writer and author of the book, *The Blessing of a Broken Heart.*

What personal qualities have helped you carry on and move in a positive direction?

That's a hard question. I really don't feel it was anything that was personal to me. I feel like it was other people — the com-

77

munity — that helped me and my family. I received so much support and love that helped me continue on and move.

I had people helping me, and they all had a special position — somebody who did our laundry, somebody who could sit and listen, and somebody who organized the food for us.

To give you an example, after Koby's murder, that first night after we got home from the cemetery (in Israel people are buried right away), my friend, Shira, made a basket for me on my bed and she put "from Your Guardian Angel." It was people who surrounded me and my immediate family who kept me going.

I've become a different person. I'm much more driven and purposeful. I have a different perspective on life.

Did you go through a period of self-pity? If so, what helped you out?

Self-pity is not the right term. When you're destroyed you don't have the strength for self-pity. I was just suffering, and sad, and destroyed. I didn't pity myself; I just had to mourn my son.

You wonder, "why you", but you know there's no answer to that question. Also living in Israel — it's different. In Hebrew you don't really have the word "pity". It's a different word. And it's a different culture.

Was there a specific moment, thought, or epiphany that helped to guide you to a better place or did it evolve?

It was a series of things that pushed me forward.

It was Koby's birthday, his fourteenth, five weeks after he was murdered. My friend, Shira, who's a grief counselor, told me I had to do something to mark his birthday. So my kids and I went into Jerusalem. We didn't know what to do. We thought we'd go out to Burger King because being kosher and moving to Israel, it was a big fun event for us to be able to eat at a kosher Burger King. But we couldn't go because it was just too sad for us. We went to a vegetarian restaurant. I got the idea to give money to beggars for Koby's birthday. The minute I got that idea a beggar came up to us in the restaurant. We gave him a lot of money. Then my kids and I went out onto the outdoor street mall and we went chasing after beggars to give to them. It was a really hard day.

But we were able to transform it into something that was fun and giving. And that's what we do. We wanted to do something Koby would like, so it's always fun.

What are your day-to-day coping skills that keep you afloat?

There's always davening (praying), learning Torah-Bible and taking care of my family. There's Shabbos (the Sabbath), yoga and walking. And writing; I'm a writer.

Torah relates us to God and God is infinite. So when I was learning and relating to something infinite, I could relate more to my son because he was in that place. Torah connects you to other worlds. The language of Torah is very pure. And that's what I felt I needed after Koby's murder. I needed something that had that "untouched" feeling.

In general, how have you managed to rebuild your life?

I received so much help and support. I wanted to give back what I had received.

My husband and I started a camp for bereaved children. We have 400 kids at the camp. We always try to do something fun and giving; to help teach people to rise from this and not be broken.

We also run programs for mothers. We have had over 25 healing retreats for different groups of mothers. I went to almost all of them. We have support groups. I've been part of a group within the Koby Mandell Foundation for the past seven years. And we keep evolving. Wednesday is Koby Mandell Foundation day in Jerusalem. We have belly dancing, yoga, psycho-drama for the women. We have programs in resilience and renewal. These are for bereaved mothers who have lost children to either terror or illness, or any form of loss. We also have a healing retreat over the summer, a bereavement retreat for Americans.

What advice would you offer someone going through tremendous difficulty, in the hope of coming out of the darkness intact?

You have to use it to grow, to be bigger. You have to basically change your life afterwards. You can't go back to who you were. You have to find a way to give from the pain.

I read something by Rabbi Soloveitchik: "Every darkness has its own secret; and sometimes God only speaks to us in the darkness." There's a message there. It's like the difference between growing in the light and growing in the darkness; there's two ways to grow, but growing in the darkness is much more common.

And language — that's another thing. Ordinary language becomes unbearable because it can't contain your experience. Like even the expression, "making lemonade from lemons" — phrases like that can't describe it. You lose your connection to a lot of people because you can't relate to what they say and the way they speak.

I think very few people talk about the language problem. They express it like they can't bear their friends and people saying the wrong things. But I don't think it's just that people say the wrong things; I think it's a matter of not having language to contain the experience. If you don't have the feeling that people are there to support you, you'll kind of begrudge what they say.

Also, grief and trauma are in the body. So you have to deal with the body, too.

> "It is when our hearts are broken that God sculpts our souls, prodding open the narrow entrances to the caves of our being. Whenever God takes from you, he has to give you something back. God has given me the blessing of a broken heart."

The Blessings of a Broken Heart *by Sherri Mandell*

୬**ಎ**

POST TRAUMATIC GROWTH (PTG), is the concept whereby we can be positively changed by our struggle with loss, adversity, or trauma. It goes beyond resilience — the ability to bounce back. PTG occurs when we create new meaning as a result of tragedy. Suffering alone doesn't bring about this growth and change; it's what we do with our pain and suffering, how we respond to it.

> *"Suffering is not necessary to find meaning; meaning is possible even in spite of suffering." (Frankl 1959)*

Viktor Frankl, a psychiatrist and neurologist from Austria, speaks to this in his profound classic, Man's Search for Meaning, in which he discusses his logotherapy — the therapy of meaning.

> *"We must never forget that we may also find meaning in life even when confronted with a hopeless situation, when facing a fate that cannot be changed. For what then matters is to bear witness to the uniquely human potential at its best, which is to transform a personal tragedy into triumph, to turn one's predicament into a human achievement. When we are no longer able to change a situation — just think of an incurable disease such as inoperable cancer — we are challenged to change ourselves." (Frankl 1959)*

Tragic loss demands that we become different as we restructure our lives around a new reality. We pick up the shattered pieces of glass that cut into us at every turn and reconfigure a life incorporating the loss.

How can we respond to our situation, to our suffering? Frankl goes on to say,

> *"Everything can be taken from a man but one thing: the*

last of the human freedoms — to choose one's attitude in any given set of circumstances, to choose one's own way."
(Frankl 1959)

Choosing to create something meaningful and helpful gives purpose to our life at a time when all seems lost and hopeless. Attaching to something outside and bigger than ourselves can pull us out of the quicksand that is threatening to swallow us up alive. It redirects our focus towards hope and renewal.

We can choose to turn pain into purpose.

Frankl, Viktor. 1959. *Man's Search for Meaning.* Boston, MA: Beacon Press

CHAPTER 9

The Vision to Keep Going Forward

"Don't let your sight get in the way of your vision."

"The real story, in my mind, isn't how I got out of the World Trade Center, it's how I got there in the first place."

Michael Hingson lets nothing get in the way of his living life to the absolute fullest. Indeed, he's had challenges, but he's taken them on as opportunities from which to grow and adapt in positive and meaningful ways.

Blind from birth, his parents encouraged him to live a "regular" life, cycling around his neighborhood (yes, you read that right — riding on a bike), attending mainstream classes and playing along with everyone else. Given this all-important foundation of "I can do it", he grew up with a fierce sense of independence and high functioning capabilities. These allowed him to adapt, cope, integrate and create a "normal" life of advanced schooling (a master's in physics), a career and marriage.

Michael miraculously survived 9/11 with the assistance of his guide dog, Roselle, as together they walked down 78 flights of stairs (1,463 steps) to safety and then ran for their lives.

He is the author of *Thunder Dog,* a best-selling memoir about his life. He's also a motivational speaker and has had a strong career in computer technology.

What personal qualities have helped you carry on and move in a positive direction?

83

I think persistence.

I think being able to focus.

And I think also the fact that I believe very strongly in teamwork. I like to feed off of other people. We all feed off of each other; sometimes we recognize it more than others.

More than anything, we all need to be self-starters and self-motivators. I just don't like to be down. I can get angry as much as the next person, but I also know it's my job to keep motivated and focused.

I love to enjoy life and do that as much as I possibly can. A lot of times I hear people saying things like, "I have to go do this speech today"; I much prefer saying, "I have this great opportunity to go do this today". If you adopt this kind of mind-set, it helps you have a much more positive outlook.

You have to set the stage for yourself. If you don't do it, somebody else will, and then if you don't like the stage or the players on the stage you have nobody else to blame but yourself because you didn't make the choice; or the choice you made was to be inactive.

Did you go through a period of self-pity? If so, what helped you out?

I don't think there is any one of us who, at one point or another in our life, doesn't go through some form of self-pity. The issue is how you deal with it.

One of the things that helps me usually is that when I'm down my wife isn't, and when she is, I'm not. Occasionally it happens that we both are; and after a little bit of crying time, kind of the philosophy is, "it is what it is", and I've gotta move forward, and so I come out of it. Again it gets back to "I set the stage."

You have to have control over what you do.

There are a lot of things in our lives that we don't have control over. But there also are a lot of things that we do, many of which we don't think that we do. For example, the World Trade Center happened. No doubt, we had no control over that. What I did have control over was how I dealt with what happened. Like any change in our lives, any tragedy, the positive thing we have control over is how mentally we deal with the change. That's the important thing — don't worry about the things you can't control, focus on the things you can.

Was there a specific moment or epiphany that helped guide you to a better place mentally and psychologically, or did it evolve?

It was a kind of evolution. I've also had epiphanies along the way.

Blind people typically aren't considered for jobs. The unemployment rate among employable blind people in this country, according to the social security administration, is nearly 80%. And that's not because blind people can't work; that's because people who have eyesight, or as I talk about them, "light-dependent people", tend to think we can't do stuff. They think sight is the only game in town, which is why I say in Thunderdog, "Don't let your sight get in the way of your vision."

There's always the debate — do you tell people in a resumé or cover letter that you're blind, or do you not? I've literally had interviews cancelled when I didn't mention I was blind and somebody figured it out because of things I mentioned in the resumé. I've had interviews cancelled at the last minute before I left for them.

My wife said to me once, "You took the Dale Carnegie sales course. That course always preached about turning liabilities into assets." That was an immediate epiphany and when I applied for a job, which was a sales position, the last paragraph in my cover letter basically said:

> *"The most important thing you should consider about me when you're hiring someone for this job is that I happen*

to be blind. As a blind person, I've had to sell all my life just to be able to live and function. I've had to sell just to be able to rent or buy a home, get on an airplane; so when you're hiring someone for this job do you want to hire someone who just has sales in their life as a profession or do you want to hire somebody who understands sales for the art and science that it is and has had to use it as part of his daily life 24 hours a day."

I got the job. At least I got the interview because of that and that did lead to me getting the job.

That was a pretty amazing epiphany. It is a big debate — do you say that you're blind or do you not? The reality is, there are a lot of ways to spin that for a lot of different jobs — to be able to say that I have the same qualifications and that you should consider me because I have more to bring to the job than other people. Now you have to make that point and prove it. But the fact of the matter is, in our society three out of every four people fear blindness over any other disability, according to the Gallup poll. One of the top five fears people have in this country is being blind, not physically disabled, but blind because we put such an emphasis on eyesight. So it's a real challenge. It's so very frustrating that people don't want to deal with that. We're hoping that *Thunderdog* helps.

What are your day-to-day coping skills that keep you afloat?

Relying on my wits, listening to input from other people, and smiling.

What thoughts propel you forward?

It's always about what keeps me going. The answer again is — So what am I going to do next? What opportunities are open to me right now? But I think that for me it's that I've made choices in my life that have put me in a position of needing to do things.

I have a business, and we just started Roselle's Dream Foundation to raise money to help provide technologies to blind people.

A lot of the technology we use is very expensive; and we have nearly 50% of blind people living below the poverty level because of the fact that we can't get jobs and there aren't a lot of financial resources available for us. We're talking about $5,000-$6,000 just to get something to be able to take notes on the job. We're hoping to provide scholarships and we're hoping to be able to get more money through the foundation to do that. So this keeps me busy.

So for me, part of it is I've put myself in a position of needing to move forward because that's what I do.

In general, how have you managed to rebuild your life?

Life is a constant rebuilding for all of us. Certainly after 9/11. And there have been other times where I've had challenges that have come up.

I worked for a company back in 1984 that was purchased by Xerox and they decided to get rid of all the pre-Xerox sales people, and I was the last to be let go. I looked for a job for six months and couldn't find one. Finally what I decided to do, with a friend, was start my own company.

Again, it was "What am I going to do next?" I tried a few things; they didn't work. We started doing the Cad (computer-aided design) systems and that kept us afloat for four years. What I learned along the way was I didn't need to operate a Cad system to be able to sell it; what I needed to know was how to run it so I could tell others what to do.

Again for a rebuild it was still dealing with the positive — you gotta do what you gotta do to move forward. And we went through a very tough financial period during that time, which is why I eventually went back to the workforce in 1989 and got a job and we've been able to move forward.

It still starts from within when you want to rebuild your life. It's your choice as to what you do.

If I were to suggest to other people what they "should" do if they're going through a tragedy or any kind of unexpected change I would say you must start with accepting the fact that the change happened, especially if you didn't have control over it. And even if you did and it took an unexpected turn where you were left in a quandary, you must start with "All right, where am I?" Get over the fact that it happened — "Now where do I go from here?" I don't care what the challenge is, we all can start with that.

We had a lot of people displaced in Hurricane Katrina. We had a lot of people killed in the World Trade Center, and I worked in the WTC on 9/11. I lost my office that day; lost the space where all of my employees worked — because I had a staff. We were suddenly left without an opportunity to go in to a place to work. What we needed to do was to figure out how to go forward. We all had laptop computers and worked from home. We worked out ways of getting together. We continued to thrive and sell above goal. That was because we made the decision to go forward and thrive.

You can wallow in self-pity or you can decide at some point "I've done enough of that, now what am I going to do?" Things may not work out as planned. We wanted to move back to California before 9/11. And that obviously didn't happen. Then after 9/11 I was offered a job to come out and work for Guide Dogs for the Blind in California to be their spokesperson. We did that. And then my job was phased out in 2008. That was an abrupt change because I expected to stay there the rest of my life; I'd been getting guide dogs from there since 1964.

I had a choice, and what I decided to do was to continue doing what they said nobody was interested in doing and nobody was interested in hearing about, and that was continuing to tell my story and to be motivating. And so I started my own company to do that. We found a couple of other sources to help with income and we've moved forward.

For me it's always a matter of "what do I do about it?" Well, we've moved forward and we're moving on. We got *Thunderdog* published. It's been a New York Times bestseller, and it was number one on e-books for New York Times on the bestseller list. We started a foundation to help other people, which is very small right now, but we're hoping to raise money for it. I literally travel the world speaking about trust and teamwork and moving on after change.

What advice do you have for others going through difficult situations?

Don't worry about the things you can't control; focus on the things you can and the rest will take care of itself.

Reference:

Thunder Dog: The True Story of a Blind Man, His Guide Dog, and the Triumph of Trust by Michael Hingson

❦

So much of what happens to us is out of our control. Do we succumb to it, throw up our hands and proclaim surrender and victimization? (None of these interviewees do.) Charles Swindoll, pastor and educator says, "I am convinced that life is 10% what happens to me and 90% how I react to it." Oftentimes it seems like some people are just born that way and can automatically bounce back with a smile on their face, forging ahead no matter what comes their way. It seems so natural for them, but we look at them and think, "I could never be like that." It's true we may have a natural bias towards seeing the glass as either half empty or half full, but even the more pessismistic among us can raise the level in the glass if we adopt purposeful, intentional behaviors and develop a mindset of growth and change.

Sonja Lyubomirsky, psychologist and researcher, came up with a pie chart to show the components of happiness. She states in her chart that only 10% of our happiness is connected to circumstance, 40% is our intentional behaviors and 50% is genetically based. Now 40% is a lot to have in our control, and that's what we need to focus on.

As Abraham Lincoln said, "Most folks are as happy as they make up their minds to be."

As creators and authors of our lives we have control over how we deal with what happens to us.

To instill in someone an "I can do it" attitude is truly a gift, which Mr. Hingson's parents certainly gave to him. They understood there was no room for pity. Pity only produces a further crippling of someone's personality on top of whatever disability they may have. To impose limits on someone is like putting them in a small pen with high walls. There's nowhere to go. We must be aware of our own beliefs as we impart them to our vulnerable children. The words we say are the transporters of those powerful messages. The words "can" and "can't" are two small words that carry huge ramifications.

Here are a few examples from my own experience:

➤ Despite my daughter Nava's stuttering, I encouraged her to order her own food in restaurants. The last thing I wanted was her stuttering to impinge and stifle her beautifully outgoing and friendly personality. Obviously it would have been faster and easier if I ordered for her. But what an awful message that would send, which she would internalize: "I can't do it, I'm not capable, I can't order for myself; someone else has to do it for me." And what does that eventually yield? Dependency, crippling, incompetency and a lousy sense of self — the exact opposite of what I wanted her to grow into!

➤ She would make her own phone calls — no easy task for someone who has fluency difficulties.

➤ Despite her difficulty getting in and out of our mini-van, and to my mother's overt dismay at my watching her struggle and not running to help her, she climbed in and out by herself. And if anyone would attempt to give her a hand, she'd say, "No, I can do it myself." And she'd feel good about it, and proud of herself.

We all have way more potential than we realize, and probably more than we'll ever actualize. However, encouraging someone to be the best and most they can be, to watch as those flower petals open to their fullest extent, is giving them the gift of their most able and engaged life. We're here to bring forth our best selves to the life we've been given. A "can-do" attitude facilitates this expansion.

Lyubomirsky, Sonja. 2008. *The How of Happiness: A New Approach to Getting the Life You Want.* New York: Penguin Press.

"It is not what we expect from life, but rather what life expects from us."

Viktor Frankl

CHAPTER 10

"I Can" — The Fuel of Life

"Without the valley, there can be no mountain peaks."

 Glenda Watson Hyatt has taken the "least obvious path" and become a motivational speaker. Why is this something special and unique? Because Ms. Hyatt has cerebral palsy, which affects her speech to a significant degree. Her physical movements are jerky and involuntary and she walks with support. "Can't" was not a word used in her household growing up. She clearly took this lesson to heart and is, therefore, a most inspiring teacher in modeling an "I can do" way of life.

What personal qualities have helped you carry on and move forward in a positive direction?

My determination and perseverance help to keep me moving forward. I do what it takes to get the job done — whether it's spending seven years to complete my Bachelor of Arts, taking four years to write my autobiography, *I'll Do It Myself,* or creating a technology mashup to speak publicly even with a speech impairment. And when someone says I can't do something, it adds fuel to my fire and makes me more determined to get the job done and to prove them wrong.

My optimism keeps me focused on what I can do and what I do have, rather than on what I am lacking. I might have a significant speech impairment, but that isn't stopping me from becoming a motivational speaker.

My creativity allows me to come up with solutions that enable me to circumvent an obstacle; for example, by using a Gorilla tripod to mount my camera to my scooter, I can now enjoy photography as a hobby.

Did you go through a period of self-pity? If so, what helped lift you out?

Generally I am a happy, cheerful person. But to be honest, I do have a momentary pity-party-for-one on the rare occasion. In the really tough moments, I think about my Nanna (my Mom's mom) who had bone cancer. She crawled up and down her old wood stairs to do the laundry in the basement. When needed, I draw upon her inner strength. If she could manage to do that to get the job done, then I can deal with my momentary frustration or pain.

In the end, I see my cerebral palsy (and how others treat me because of it) as something that is. No amount of crying and self-pity is going to change that fact. I might as well get on with it and make the most of what I do have. There is so much I can do; I try to focus on that.

Was there a specific moment or epiphany that helped to guide you to a better place mentally and psychologically, or did it evolve over time?

From my earliest memories I have generally had a positive and determined attitude. Granted, some days require more of a conscientious effort to remain positive. Some days I need to accept that without the valley, there can be no mountain peaks — and that is OK. Those valleys make the peaks sweeter, something to cherish even more.

What are your day-to-day coping skills that keep you afloat?

In terms of keeping afloat day-to-day, I use a variety of coping skills, depending upon what I need in that moment. When I get slightly discouraged, I focus on what I do have and what I can do. Coming across a story about someone living their passion lights my fire and gets me going again. Likewise, listening to one of my favorite songs that hold special meaning to me boosts my energy to keep me going. To recharge and to have space to think and to regroup, I take time off and go do something I enjoy; even a nap with my kitty can be enough of a break to refresh. And, when needed, I accept that my day did not go as intended, as planned, and that is OK. I get to try again tomorrow.

What thoughts propel you forward?

Even though I am beyond tired at times and feel like coasting for a while, I hear that little voice in my head say, "Wait! I am not done trying. There is still so much more I want to do or to accomplish." That little voice keeps me going, moving forward, to discover what else I can add to the "Yes, I can" column of my life.

In general, how have you managed to push through your limitations and build a rich and successful life? (Perhaps you can define what "success" means to you.)

To me, success means working with my limitations or finding ways around them to lead a happy and fulfilled life. This means finding a balance between appreciating and being grateful for what I do have in that moment while still trying to improve my situation. Oftentimes it means getting creative to get something done or to increase my potential. For example, even though I have created a way to deliver a presentation to an audience, which in itself is amazing, and I am truly grateful to have that ability added to my repertoire, I will continue striving for a more graceful technical solution to deliver my message. For me that would be success.

What advice can you offer someone going through challenging or {perceived} limiting circumstances with the hope of living a good life?

You are not alone. Reach out to those around you, either in person or online. Draw on their strength, support and love. It is a sign of courage and strength to ask for help. Focus on what you have, on what you can do, and move forward from there.

I'll Do It Myself by Glenda Watson Hyatt

ع‌

THERE'S LOTS OF TALK AND RESEARCH on the importance of character strengths and emotional intelligence as they affect success and happiness. Some even say they're more significant than academics and IQ in predicting and guiding us towards success. (Of course, we have to define success for ourselves.) Angela Duckworth, scientist at the University of Pennsylvania, has been studying the trait known as grit. Grit is the ability to maintain interest and effort towards achieving one's goals, as well as the ability to persevere through tough times. She has found that character is as important as IQ. Others such as Paul Tough, journalist and author of How Children Succeed, and Julie Lythcott-Haims, former Stanford University dean and author of How To Raise An Adult, write about the importance of focusing on character traits and working on developing them as much as the academic subjects. "Character counts" is both a common saying and a program seen in many schools and communities.

We can all think of people we know who are very smart and yet don't seem to be doing too well in life. They're underachievers, afraid of failing and therefore doing far less than they're capable of. They may lack confidence, have difficulty getting along on a job, aren't flexible or resourceful, or lack problem-solving skills. It's these exact traits that push us along in life and can get us farther ahead than we think. The ability to keep getting up after falling and failing can be the difference between making it or not. The traits of perseverance, tenacity, and grit keep us on track, pushing us forward. The old "A is for effort" is not for slouches. It's for all of us to keep on, keepin' on. Michelangelo said:

"The greatest danger for most of us is not that our aim is too high and we miss it but that it is too low and we reach it."

The "can do" attitude is not one of intellect but of character that encompasses the very traits discussed in these last two interviews. Both of the interviewees speak of persistence, perseverance, and the ability to stay focused and goal-oriented. This, in itself, entails self-discipline, creativity and resourcefulness — the capacity to think outside of the box when problem-solving.

Character strengths can be cultivated. We can work to enhance our stick-to-itiveness towards that special something we want. In writing this book, I had to draw on my self-discipline and perseverance to do this project that is very meaningful to me. This book is my way of getting my passion and life's motif — transcending adversity and living well despite — out there into the world via my interviews. I found myself procrastinating and finding everything else to do first before sitting down to write; and then oops, no time to write today.... I am constantly pushing through my resistance of it not being good enough, as my internal voice nags at me all too often. This is my inner chatter and struggle and I must call upon my strengths of love of learning and grit to keep me going and stay on course.

Breaking through our limitations takes strength of character. Both of these interviewees have clearly pushed beyond their inherent challenges. The word and concept of limit is a self-imposed mindset of what we decide we can and cannot do. I recently heard someone present publicly at a large rally. He prefaced his speech by saying that he has Tourette's syndrome and that he will be making frequent and uncontrollable odd sounds throughout his speech. What a brilliant strategy — to prime his audience so that we all knew right away to expect something out of the norm and thereby not be completely thrown off. We were then able to look beyond it and focus on his message. One would think, how could someone with a pretty severe speech impediment engage in public speaking? Why put himself out there displaying his weak spot where it manifests the most — in speaking! And yet why not? It's usually our own embarrassment, fear and stigma that holds us back and prevents us from engaging, which only imprisons us into our own small and limiting holding cell.

> *"Men are not prisoners of fate, but only prisoners of their own minds." Franklin D. Roosevelt*

What limitation(s) have you put upon yourself from which you could push through?

Think about your strengths and then take the 20-minute free survey (link under Resources) and see how the calculated top five signature strengths compare to how you see yourself. Then start being more intentional of using them in your everyday life.

Resources

List of the 24 character strengths:
https://www.apu.edu/strengthsacademy/pdfs/character_strengths_virtues_descriptions.pdf

Take the free VIA Survey (Click the button on the right):
http://www.viacharacter.org/www/Character-Strengths/VIA-Classification

Reference List

Duckworth, Angela. 2016. Grit: The Power of Passion and Perseverance. New York: Scribner

Lythcott-Haims, Julie. 2015. *How to Raise an Adult: Break Free of the Overparenting Trap and Prepare Your Kid for Success.* New York: St. Martin's Press

Tough, Paul. *How Children Succeed: Grit, Curiosity, and the Hidden Power of Character.* New York: Houghton Mifflin Harcourt

Chapter 11

The Stroke of Luck

"What I need to do is impact someone in a positive way every single day."

Out of thin air, boom, your life as you know it is gone. You wake up to a completely unfamiliar and scary version of you. Chances are you might want to roll over (if you could) and die right there. But you can't; you're trapped, and in a seemingly different body.

Julia Fox Garrison is a very funny woman who has rebuilt her life after suffering a near fatal stroke at the age of 37. She is now an author, motivational speaker and patient advocate. Her book, *Don't Leave Me This Way Or When I Get Back On My Feet You'll Be Sorry,* attests to her witty, finding-the-humor-in-everything personality.

"Your attitude is the only control you have left in your life — that and your nail polish color, of course."

What personal qualities have helped you carry on and move in a positive direction?

I use humor to cope. I grew up in a family of eight brothers and no sisters — the only girl of nine. I think that prepared me for what I was going to face in my future. You can't be a shrinking violet in that type of dynamic.

I'm very strong, and I get my strength from all the support around me. I feel that I've been given qualities by God. My faith is what sustained me through the really tough times. I was never one to say, "poor me". I hate the word "pity".

Did you go through a period of self-pity?

I never ever said "Why me?" It was always, "This happened to me, let's move on. What do I need to do?" I talk about pity parties in my presentations. It's important to have a pity party to acknowledge my sadness so that I could make progress, move forward and not get stuck. I had them at night when no one was around as far as crying and trying to figure out where to go from here. I did suffer; not feeling sorry for myself, but I went through an identity crisis. I was in the corporate world climbing the corporate ladder, and then a day later I'm fighting for my life, having brain surgery, coming out of that totally paralyzed on my left side. I couldn't even feed myself, or go to the bathroom on my own without three nurses lifting me. Losing my personal independence and who I was pre-stroke were the things I felt sad about, but I never felt "Why me?" I know that not having that feeling was not normal and that it was a divine gift.

What I asked of people when they came to see me was not to come in and say, "Oh, poor Julia. Oh I'm sorry this happened", because pity is really a worthless emotion. It does nothing for the recipient; it might be an emotional reaction for the person giving it but it's not helpful. I made every effort to create an upbeat, positive and happy atmosphere in my hospital room (where I was for several months). I created my very own dichotomy. I know it may have been a façade — of course it was, because there I was drooling with a face like a melted candle — but I felt it changed the air of the room and made me not feel like I was in a dire setting. So everybody who came across my threshold knew they had to bring a good joke. My room was always full of laughter. I used to get in trouble with the hospital staff because they were always saying, "Is that room having another party?" Because there would be so much laughter and that's not a normal thing in a rehab setting.

Did you have a strong support system in place? If so, how did that help you?

First of all, my son, Rory, turned three-years-old just a few days prior to my stroke. He has always been my little "sonshine" of inspiration. He was the primary reason I worked even harder than I thought possible.

I never ate one hospital meal, except for breakfast. Every meal was provided by my family. Each of my brothers had a day that they came in, sat with me and physically fed me. And my parents were phenomenal. People who read my book think I made up my husband because he's so good. I couldn't have written him as good as he is. He's the kindest, purest, gentlest soul — he and my mother — I think I married my mother. My husband is my left side that doesn't work anymore. I feel like I can never complain because I've been given so much.

I've done a lot of radio shows and one host asked me, "You've been given so much support, what do you say to the people who don't have that?" I thought for a second and felt, 'Geeze he just threw me under the bus because we were live on the air.' Yeah, there are people who don't have as much as I've been given and blessed with, but I think it's about the choices you make in your life. Hopefully the choices I made prior to my stroke were what helped foster the positive relationships I had, and I didn't do a one-sided relationship with people. I always tried to give as much as I could of myself.

Was there a specific moment or epiphany that helped to guide you to a better place mentally and psychologically, or did it evolve over time?

After my brain surgery, the first words I said when I came to were, "I have a purpose. There's a reason I am here; and I may never know that purpose but there is a reason." It has evolved in the sense that I thought I would never learn what that purpose was, but I do know it now. Every person on this earth has a purpose but not everyone gets to discover what it is. Mine has come full circle for me. What I need to do is impact someone every single day.

During my emergency surgery, I had a vision of a girl climbing a ladder and the ladder had no beginning or end. This ladder represented my relationship with God; and I instinctively knew that I could stay on that rung or come back, albeit in a broken body (and I did ask for Beyoncé's body but He said no, clearly), and just keep working and climbing the rungs toward becoming a better person.

Five years prior to my stroke I had a dream that I was going to be in a wheelchair and that I was going to be a better person in this wheelchair. I think we all have some kind of intuitive projection of what can happen to us in the future; we just have to open to it and pay attention to it. I do pay attention to my dreams now; I'm looking for that lottery one now!

I am so wealthy in the lottery of life. I would never trade my life for anyone else's.

What are your day-to-day coping skills that keep you afloat?

Every day I get up I say thank you for another day. I truly feel that every day is a gift. It's so cliché, but it's so true. I have gratitude for everything. I think we cannot have enough gratitude for things and abilities we take for granted.

Humor is my vehicle for getting through the day. My left-side neglect can get me in a lot of trouble. My brain doesn't realize I have a left side; I've had some great fun with some of the predicaments it's gotten me into, often leaving folks bewildered and bemused.

It's a choice — do I want to survive or be a victim. I don't want to be a victim. Victims are underground. Everything is based on a choice.

For me happiness is a choice that must become a habit, so it happens naturally. That sounds so simple and basic but it takes a lot of effort. Some days happiness doesn't land in your lap, you have to really work at it. We all have moments of happiness, but I have come to realize to sustain happiness it has to have a foundation — my happiness is rooted in gratitude as well as forgiveness... to give up what I cannot control and some of that is my own body betraying me, so I had to forgive myself.

One of my biggest life lessons is I've learned not to be embarrassed. Embarrassment is what I think other people think of me, but I am not a mind-reader so I learned embarrassment was my internal voice, not an external one of opinion. Nobody can judge me but God. So I'm free-spirited now. It has made me a lighter person in how I view things. When I'm true to myself I'm true to others.

I celebrate my 'homage to my hemorrhage' every year (July 17th); I have a party. It's a day of reflection and of gratitude for these extra years. Actually, I celebrate every day because I learned the hard way that awaking each day is not guaranteed, it is a bonus. When people ask, how I can celebrate such a horrific day, I say, "That gives me power over it."

What advice would you offer someone going through a rough situation, so they can come out intact?

It's all about choosing the attitude on how you approach it. My motto is 'positive outlook equals positive outcome'. If you illuminate the positives, you'll get more positive outcomes. It doesn't mean the problems go away; they're still there, but only in the shadows. They're not getting as much power. What you concentrate on is magnified and becomes more powerful. I know that the quality of my life is an inside job.

I never talk about my deficits; it's clear I have them but I don't talk about them. I don't think of myself as handicapped and that gives me a lot more freedom. If I think of myself that way, then I've handicapped my mind. And then I've handicapped my family, and it spreads. As a person surrounded by loved ones, those people are affected by everything I do. So it is up to me to set the tone, so I choose to be upbeat and positive.

One of my other messages that I think is important for anybody is to perform simple acts of kindness daily. When people think of doing something for another, they always think of it as something grand and sophisticated; but kindness is really straightforward and not sophisticated. Sometimes it is as simple as smiling. Smiles are free and need no translation. I have found that when I leave a trail of smiles behind, it paves the path ahead with wonderful possibilities and positive connections. It is easy to get caught up in routines and lose sight of humanity. That's what we're on this earth to do — to help each other.

I think we are conditioned to say the word 'can't' which closes all doors to possibilities. I have discovered that if you include the word 'yet' then the door to opportunity remains ajar. I used to say 'can't' so often that it became second nature in conversation. Now I avoid saying 'can't', but when I need to say it, I always include the qualifier, 'yet'. So I can't rollerblade yet, but I plan on it someday, maybe.

Don't Leave Me This Way by Julia Fox Garrison

꿈

THERE IS MUCH RESEARCH TODAY ON THE BENEFITS OF HUMOR and laughter. Humor is a coping tool, a stress buster and an overall wonderful ingredient that contributes to our well-being. Norman Cousins, journalist and professor, used humor and laughter to nurse himself back to health as he wrote about in his book, Anatomy of An Illness.

Humor and laughter improve our immune system, release those good endorphins that give us relief from pain, elevate our mood, and reduce anxiety. There are now thousands of laughter clubs throughout the world, inspired by Dr. Kataria who started them in India in the mid 1990's. Laughter exercises that start off with forced laughter quickly turn to contagious, deep body-shaking laughter, the kind where you grab onto your stomach as tears fall down your cheeks.

"A person without a sense of humor is like a wagon without springs. It's jolted by every pebble on the road."
Henry Ward Beecher

Humor cuts the tension and brings instant relief, giving us that break away from the seriousness of the situation as Ms. Fox Garrison clearly shows us. Of course, not all of us are innately funny or able to find the humor in ordinary situations, let alone terrible ones. But it would be helpful if we could step outside the intensity and look for some of the ludicrousness, if only for a quick shift in perspective or an instantaneous tension buster. And those embarrassing moments can certainly teach us to laugh at ourselves.

We know that what we focus on moves into the forefront of our reality. Focusing on the positive, finding humor, and honing in on what we can do versus what we can't, puts us in a better position to pick up the pieces of our lives and create new meaning with the new version of ourselves. It doesn't take away the problem, of course, and we're not looking to be 'Pollyanna-ish' about it, but it widens our lens so we can see the good and be open to the possibilities as well.

Check out a laughter club in your area. It may just be the kind of break you need from a challenging situation, and would be a unique and fun gift to yourself:

http://www.worldlaughtertour.com/clubs/premier-directory/ ;
http://laughteryoga.org/find-club/

Reference List

Cousins, Norman. 1979. *Anatomy of an Illness: As Perceived by the Patient*. New York: W.W. Norton & Company.

"Everything can be taken from a man but one thing: the last of the human freedoms — to choose one's attitude in any given set of circumstances, to choose one's own way."

Viktor Frankl

CHAPTER 12

A Family Affair

"You can't live your life on the 'what ifs.'"

Meredith Vieira is a journalist and TV personality. She was the original talk show host of The View and co-hosted the Today show, the NBC early morning news program, as well as the game show, *Who Wants to Be a Millionaire.* She hosted her own talk show, *The Meredith Vieira Show on NBC.* She continues to be a news correspondent for NBC.

The issue I focused on with Ms. Vieira is one that is unfortunately all too prevalent — that of chronic illness, caregiving and its impact upon the family. Richard Cohen, Ms. Vieira's husband, has been living with multiple sclerosis for more than 30 years. Mr. Cohen is a TV producer and writer. He writes a reflective and insightful column on chronic illness for AARP Magazine. He has also written a couple of books. It becomes a 'family affair' to live and cope with the daily struggles and difficulties of a chronic and debilitating condition. The challenge here is to live as best as one can, with it and despite it; and Ms. Vieira and Mr. Cohen do it well together.

What personal qualities have helped you carry on and move in a positive direction?

For me what has helped is for Richard to be open about his illness. For a very long time he was closed. Partly that was out of concern about how people would react to him, professionally and personally. He kept his disease from people. That made it harder to deal with as a couple. You knew you were part of this masking and I don't think that's healthy for the other person involved — the partner. I understood it and I didn't force the issue, but I was glad when Richard decided to be honest with people. That was the result of our older son as a very little boy, at six or seven, asking me late one night when the lights were off in his room, "What's the matter with Dad?" Kids are so smart. I don't remember what I said exactly in the moment to comfort him — something like that Dad was fine and in the morning we'd all talk about it. The next day we did; we explained it in terms a child could understand. It was after that that Richard realized, "I want to be open about this now." So I think the openness has helped me. I'm all for not burying feelings. I think it's much better to get it out.

A sense of humor: We both have a pretty good sense of humor. We can laugh at the absurd. And when you have this kind of illness, there are moments that are really absurd. You can either get very depressed, which is understandable, or you can try to shake it off as best you can, put it in perspective and move on. I think humor helps us put things in perspective. That has been a great coping mechanism for me as well as for Richard. He often will lead the way. He'll have an episode where maybe he drops something and he gets very angry at himself. And then he'll make a joke; and that allows me, that gives me permission to make a joke back. Nine times out of ten we reach that point, and I think that has been tremendously helpful.

Friends: This comes with openness. I am totally comfortable leaning on friends. We have wonderful friends who not only ask Richard how he is doing, but will ask me how I'm doing. This speaks to the whole notion of family illness. This is an important message, if I was to get out anything, it is — for those who know someone with chronic illness — 'don't be afraid to ask'. We appreciate it. A lot of people are scared to bring it up because they may feel they're walking on egg shells around people who are chronically ill. My experience has been that most people in that situation like when it's acknowledged and they have that opportunity to speak about it.

Did you go through a period of self-pity? If so, what helped lift you out?

Sure I have days when Richard will say Why me?' and I'll say to myself, 'Why me?' I knew about Richard's illness before I married him; it wasn't sprung on me. He was diagnosed with MS when he was 25. And I married him when I was 33. He's five years older than me.

We used to run all the time together. We can't do that anymore. I love things like skiing — things that he can't do. There are moments when we're talking about a vacation and we're limited and then I'll feel, 'Oh I really want to do that'. It's one of those passing things. But I also think that's OK. It's OK to have a pity party every once in a while, just let it out. Because there is loss — there's physical loss and emotional loss. There's that kind of day-to-day loss, and it's alright to feel bad about that as long as you can put it in perspective; in the scheme of things that 'ain't' the biggest issue.

Please speak here to the issue of caretaking.

"Caregiver" is the word I use. Richard is not in the position where he needs that kind of attention. Because he has secondary MS, he has less ability to use his hands and eyesight than he used to. So there are times when I am his hands or his sight — for reading a menu, tying a shoe or doing that top button on a shirt. But I'm certainly not a full-time caregiver. We sort of take care of each other.

I think a lot of people who are caregivers feel tremendous guilt when they allow their personal feelings to rise above those of their spouse. It's sort of like 'How dare you? That's the person who's ill, not you; so what right do you have?' And I think you have every right, whatever your emotions are.

Was there a specific moment or epiphany that helped to guide

you to a better place mentally and psychologically, or did it evolve?

I understood enough about MS going into the marriage in part because my dad was a doctor. I went to appointments with Richard and I saw people younger than him who were already wheelchair-bound. I knew the potential progression of the illness. It's so unpredictable. Will Richard end up in a wheelchair or worse — bedridden? Is it possible? Sure it is, but we have no way of knowing what's going to be the outcome. Every individual is different. I knew a possible trajectory of the illness heading into it. It sounds so trite, but that expression about being hit by a bus tomorrow — you just don't know in life. He could dive off a diving board and break his neck and be a quadriplegic. I could get ill. You can't live your life on the 'what ifs', because you'd never do anything. So to me it was worth it.

This is just a part of what we deal with. Everybody has their stuff. This is our stuff.

There's that wonderful story of everyone putting their troubles in a bag and throwing them all in a pile, and all you want is your own bag back. Because it's familiar.

Richard especially has had a bum deal because he also has had two bouts of colon cancer. It hasn't only been MS for him. I did have a little conversation with God after the second bout of cancer. I said, "Really, really, this guy doesn't deserve all this." I thought that was a cheap shot giving him extra suffering, just really unnecessary. We had already gotten the lesson.

Take away that part of our life and there are unbelievable pluses. It's led Richard to a point in terms of his own reflection where he was able to write two beautiful books about chronic illness. Write what you know. And help people. His books have really helped people. To be able to have that gift where you can actually change somebody's life, that's a pretty amazing gift. It came at a cost, but it's still an amazing gift.

When he wrote about it, he was able to release and let go. I think it was very empowering for him and I think it gave him a strength he didn't have before. MS does a real number on you where you feel like less of a man. This gave him some of his self-worth back. It allowed him to articulate it. He had buried it. When he started to write about it, it helped him deal better with his illness and face it. He talks a lot about denial and he thinks denial is a very good thing. For the longest time he denied the illness and said, "I don't care; they say I can't be a producer, I'll be a producer." It worked for him up to a certain point, but by burying it he wasn't allowing himself to feel everything he needed to feel and to face everything he needed to face.

Writing his first book, his memoir, Blindsided, allowed him to do it in a safe way because he is a writer. It was like therapy. His second book, Strong at the Broken Places, is a profile of five people with chronic illness. His third book has nothing to do with illness. It's called, I Want to Kill the Dog. It's hysterical. It's about our history with our pets in our family. It's freedom again. He said, "I don't want to be known just as the disability author. There's more to me." He's almost come full circle. "MS doesn't totally define me; it's part of my life, it's not all of my life." He's a very funny guy and so he wrote this very funny book.

Any specific day-to-day coping skills?

I just kind of live day-to-day. Today was a good day or maybe today wasn't the best day, but tomorrow might be better. That seems to work best for me. We're still in that stage where that's doable. When you are living with any kind of illness, you really learn to appreciate the here and now. It takes on an added value because you're lucky to have it. If there's any coping mechanism that's what it is: try to be as much in the moment as you can be and enjoy it; or understand if it's not great, then this too shall pass.

What advice would you offer people going through their own difficult situation?

In our family it has been sense of humor and honesty.

It's important to be able to communicate. Illness is a family affair. You need to keep the communication going and open on all sides. And certainly if you have kids as well. As I said, keeping this from our kids was a little off because kids in general are so attuned to things.

Build that group of friends, that support system around you. Go for it. Don't be afraid. Don't feel that you're a burden to other people. And don't be ashamed of illness. What you'll discover is everybody else has their own thing. People don't like to talk about stuff. They hide it, but if you're open and you say you need help, people will be there for you. It's important to know they're there. It's like it takes a village; when there's illness it takes a village too. Most people have been phenomenal.

~

CAREGIVERS NEED THEIR OWN SUPPORT — guilt-free support. They're an entity unto themselves. They've often gone through the loss of the person as he/she used to be. That's a grief process in and of itself. But the caregiver doesn't have the time to grieve when they're trying to do it all. They have to cope with the magnitude of responsibilities and keep all the balls in the air.

It's common to feel guilty for feeling bad, for being tired, for wanting a life outside the sick. But it's exactly in taking care of ourselves that we, the caregiver, can be at our best. We cannot run on empty; we must fill our own bucket too so we can continue giving. It's obviously hard to find the time, but we must take the time. And that's where asking for help comes in — to help the neglected caregiver.

It's important to let our guard down, at least to ourselves, and allow ourselves to crawl into that deep hole. It may feel scary, like how will we ever get out if we let ourselves in? But it's in having that lick-our-wounds time where we cry our eyes out, scream into the mattress, hide under the covers and don't come out until we're all cried out, that can actually bring us back in a more restored way. We need to give ourselves permission to fall apart and then put ourselves back together again — unlike Humpty Dumpty.

We also need to be real with getting support. There's no place for martyrdom when dealing with major hardships. Putting on the bravado costume, appearing like we need nothing and can handle it all, puts more strain on ourselves and drains us of the good energy needed to handle the real deal.

Being vulnerable is not easy, but it's the only way to truly connect and have the opportunity to get what we need. Asking for, and gathering support is a strength.

Some people perceive crying as a weakness; asking for help is often seen the same way. In reality, it couldn't be further from the truth. Crying is a heart-felt expression of emotion and allowing ourselves to feel and express our real and deepest emotions is a sign of strength. There's no shame in feeling sad, pained and deeply hurt, as the same goes for asking for help.

When I'm feeling bad inside, I know I need to talk it out with a close friend. That's helpful for me. And so I call one of my good-listening friends and say I need to talk.

What kind of support helps you? Ask for it.

Reference List

Cohen, Richard M. 2004. *Blindsided: Lifting a Life Above Illness: A Reluctant Memoir.* New York: HarperCollins

Cohen, Richard M. 2008. *Strong at the Broken Places: Voices of Illness, a Chorus of Hope.* New York: HarperCollins

*"Death ends life,
not a relationship."*

Morrie Schwartz
Tuesdays With Morrie

CHAPTER 13

The Death of a Young Spouse

Losing a spouse is devastating; losing a spouse suddenly at the start of one's life together is tragic. Being new to adulthood, love and responsibilities is certainly not the time when thoughts of sickness, death, or loss enter one's mind. It's supposed to be a time of feeling invincible and seeing your whole life ahead of you. And then boom! Your world comes crashing down as the love of your life suddenly dies. It just isn't supposed to go this way.

These next two interviewees share this common loss of their young husbands' sudden deaths. Hope and optimism play a big role as they eventually come to see, after much heartache, that there can be light again after darkness. But they first sink into their soul-wrenching sadness and despair. To get through this they must experience all the raging feelings of grief. And they go through it head on, confronting their demons of suffering.

"Pain is inevitable; suffering is optional."

Anonymous

You're Not Going to Feel This Way Forever

"Wherever I go, there I am."

"I've reached a place where I can say that grief is not about recovery or resolution or being fully healed. It's about living without someone, but still embracing life."*

Natalie Taylor is a young woman who has unfortunately learned about the fragility of life way too early — at the beginning of her married life. While pregnant with her first child, Natalie's husband, Josh, died suddenly in a tragic carveboarding (skateboarding) accident.

Ms. Taylor's book, *Sign of Life*, is her powerfully written memoir of her journey through sadness and joy, grief and hope, as she finds the strength and courage to rebuild her life with her son, Kai.

What personal qualities have helped you carry on and move forward in a positive direction?

One thing was that my husband was so excited about life and he was just really enthusiastic and spontaneous and lived in the moment. And after he passed away I was so sad all the time. After a while I realized that this is not how he would want me to live, so I tried to channel his energy of appreciating even the smallest opportunities we get. I tried to force myself to appreciate the moment, not take for granted the time I have with my son.

The other thing is that my family has done a really good job of always asserting throughout my childhood this idea of work ethic, which sounds really weird next to grief. It doesn't matter if you have to go to plan B, you go to plan B. You do whatever you have to do to keep going, to survive, to get your head in the right place. No matter what I've ever participated in, whether I played soccer or was on a team or taking graduate courses, I always told myself, maybe I'm not the smartest person in the room or on the field, or maybe I'm not the most talented, but I can always be the person who works the hardest. I feel like I really had to do a lot of work with grieving. I made myself go to a psychologist; I made myself write even when I didn't want to. All of those things paid off; not immediately because nothing pays off immediately. But I think over time they were very helpful.

Did you go through a period of self-pity? If so, what helped lift you out of it?

It was never a prolonged period, but I definitely felt sorry for myself. Growing up, my mom had this slogan, "Get out of the pity pool". If something didn't go our way, she'd say, "You have to get out of the pity pool." I tried to keep that in mind. I do think the pity pool is never a popular place; nobody wants to be there with you. So I tried to stay out of it. I never vocalized my self-pity. I would think about it or write about it, but I would never call anyone and say "I feel sorry for myself". I would get frustrated and go for a walk or listen to a radio show, or try to get my mind off of myself because I knew that wasn't a good place to be. But sometimes I had to come to terms with thoughts like, 'You guys, or X family has everything and I have nothing I wanted, and isn't that horrible.'

Was there a specific moment or epiphany that helped guide you to a better place mentally and psychologically? Or did it evolve?

It was like collecting pebbles. One thing would happen and I'd put it in my bag and feel, 'alright'. And I'd just find more and more moments that were encouraging. For example, the first night I spent alone in my house, which was pretty early on, I woke up the next morning and said, "I'm OK I did it; nothing happened, the world didn't come to an end." And that was encouraging, especially because I was not a very independent person before all this. Any milestone I hit, like figuring out how to hang pictures with a hammer or drive my son up north by myself was encouraging. I completed a triathlon in August 2008, just over a year after losing Josh. It was a huge milestone for me. You know — my husband passed away, I was 24 and I felt like, 'My life is over, I won't progress after this, I have nothing going for me in the future.' So finishing the triathlon reminded me of a couple of things: I am very young and I do have a lot of potential that I don't know about; the future can hold exciting opportunities for me.

What are your day-to-day coping skills that keep you afloat?

One thing I try to say to myself when I hit a bad patch is this idea that 'it will pass.' I won't feel this way the whole day or the whole week. So I sort of embrace it and go through it because it will pass. It's not that I ignore it. When I do get sad I remind myself that I'll be happy again, eventually, or I'll do something else in the day that will make me happy. I just know that things change quickly, although with grief they don't change so quickly. At this point, four years out, my day-to-day attitude is so much more positive than it was three or four years ago obviously. When I do bump into things I say to myself, "It's OK, you're not going to feel this way forever."

This has also taught me that when good things happen they should be celebrated and shared because you don't know when the next bad thing will come. And you never want to say, "Gosh, I wish we would've had dinner together or I wish we would've taken the time to go over and say congratulations to that person." I try to embrace those moments of happiness because they're really important.

Even with birthdays or holidays where I would roll my eyes at them, now I say, "Come on, this is a big deal, you never know who's last Christmas this will be or how many more of these we have left, so why not make a big deal out of it?"

What thoughts propel you forward?

One thought I try to hold onto is the mantra, 'wherever I go, there I am', just to be there and appreciate what's happening. That helps me because as a single mom I always feel like I'm juggling plates. It's easy to get caught up in the, 'Oh come on we've gotta go, hurry, hurry.' I try to tell myself, wherever I go, I'm there and I have to be 100% there if I want to get anything out of that situation. It's so important because when I'm with my students I want to be 100% their teacher, and when I'm with my son I want to be 100% his mom.

I have a wonderful dad who was very much the disciplinarian. I feel like I didn't prepare myself to be the disciplinarian of the equation. But I think in raising my son I tell myself, people can help me if I need it. I can call my mom and have her come over and help me balance things out. Or I can have a friend come over and watch Kai while I get the kitchen clean for the first time all week. I was so resistant to ask for help because I was such a practical person. It was really hard because I felt like if I ask for help, that means I can't do it on my own. There's nothing wrong with saying, "Hey, this is really hard, can someone lend me a set of hands for an hour or so?" So I think I'm good at asking for help and I think I'm good at weighing when I'm overwhelmed; and I don't have to be a hero every day. People are so happy to help me.

What advice would you give someone going through a difficult time in their life?

People would tell me all the time that time can help; and I would always say, "You can stick time where the sun doesn't shine." But now I cannot say enough that time has changed me in ways that I didn't anticipate. I think that's not an easy answer for anyone, and I found it to be an incredibly frustrating answer. But you have to go through it and time has to pass for serious healing to happen. I'm even looking forward to where I'll be seven years out, where I'll be ten years out because I know I'll continue to grow and change and time will continue to help me.

The other thing that really helped me was seeing a psychologist early on. My obstetrician "forced" me to go. That was huge. I would have never gone on my own because it's admitting there's something wrong with you, which is a stupid stigma we still have. And that was really helpful in ways I could never have imagined.

Another thing I did was once I had my son I started to adopt exercise into my daily regimen; and that just makes me happier in general. That was huge for me.

I signed up for a group called Team in Training which raises money for the leukemia/lymphoma society. To do something for someone else was very helpful for me because I met people who had cancer and it was good for me to meet people, not just to share stories but also to help me do a better job of appreciating my health and my son's. Just helping people in general is helpful.

Grief can be a really egocentric emotion. There's nothing right or wrong about that, it's just how it is. Helping others made me get outside of myself and learn there's a lot of other pain and suffering happening in the world.

I'm twenty-eight — I felt really old for a while, but now I feel pretty young again, so that's good.

Signs of Life by Natalie Taylor

ॐ

BEING PRESENT WITH WHERE WE ARE IS A GREAT COPING TOOL. Not looking back and not focusing on the future keeps us right here, engaged in the now. It keeps anxiety at bay and keeps us grounded. Hence, the quote by Confucius with which Jon Kabat-Zinn titled his book, "Wherever You go, There You Are". So when Ms. Taylor is with her students, she's fully with them; and when she's with her son, she's totally with him and appreciating their time together. This is mindfulness — being in the present with what we're doing. The experience becomes a lot less fleeting when we're engaged in it. The old idea of mindfulness was of a practice and concept exercised by monks on mountain tops. But Mr. Kabat Zinn has brought this mindfulness to the mainstream.

Exercise too is a great strengthener, both for the body and the mind. True, when we're down and out, the last thing we want to do is push ourselves to get out there. The cushiony mattress of our bed with its comfy comforter beckons us to stay enveloped in its grip of escape and isolation. But another type of self-care calls us to get up and out and meet the day with some fortitude.

When Nava was in her rehab hospital for nine months, I lived up there in family housing so I could be by her side each and every day, cheering her on as she worked dreadfully hard to reclaim her life. I was very conscious of the fact that I needed to maintain my health and strength — both psychologically and physically — so I could be there for her 10 hours a day. I had been an exerciser for years and so I began a walking regimen every day. Through the dead of winter, with no sidewalks to walk on, I walked along the snowy streets, nodding an emphatic 'no' to the hospital's bus drivers as they honked to give me rides back to the rehab. This was my restorative break — I needed to do this for my self-care.

How do you care for yourself through your difficulties? This is perhaps when it's needed the most and when we're most likely (understandably so) to neglect ourselves completely.

Reference List

Kabat-Zinn, John. 1994. *Wherever You Go, There You Are: Mindfulness Meditation in Everyday Life*. New York: Hyperion

Grief and Mental Strength

"Face your emotions head on."

Amy Morin had to deal with tremendous loss over a three year period. She lost her mom and then her 26-year-old husband, both suddenly. A few years later her father-in-law became ill with terminal cancer and died. As a result of all this, Amy wrote *"13 Things Mentally Strong People Don't Do"* and it went viral. She turned it into a book by the same title which was recently published. As a social worker/therapist, she brings her personal and professional skills to the specific area of resiliency-building.

What helped you carry on and move in a positive direction?

My education as a social worker and my experiences as a psychotherapist certainly taught me a lot about grief. So fortunately, I had an understanding of what to expect and what sorts of things are helpful.

I also have really supportive friends and family and a strong faith in God, which helped me deal with that pain. I always held out hope that life could get better and I knew I could create a future that I looked forward to if I used my grief to heal.

Did you go through a period of self-pity? If so, what helped lift you out?

I had many times where I experienced self-pity. But I tried to keep them brief, because deep down, I knew that feeling sorry for myself only served as a temporary distraction from the pain. Ultimately, it would only hold me back.

I was a foster parent, and shortly after my husband died, I had a foster child whose parents had both died. It was a great reminder about how fortunate I was; I had my mother until I was 23, and she had been great — the best mother I could have asked for. And although I had only been married for five years, my husband was a wonderful person and we'd had a great marriage. So I tried to focus on all the things I had to be grateful for, rather than all I had lost.

I think the most helpful thing of all, however, was choosing to celebrate my late husband's birthday with a family adventure. Rather than throw a pity party on his birthday, his family and I decided to go on an adventure each year that honored his adventurous spirit. We've done everything from riding mules into the Grand Canyon to skydiving, and it's turned his birthday into a day we look forward to each year.

Was there a specific moment or epiphany that helped guide you to a better place mentally and psychologically?

Well, there were plenty of moments that helped guide me to a better place, and I learned plenty of lessons along the way. After the death of my mother, I really focused on developing the healthiest habits possible to deal with my pain.

But then, when my husband passed away, I realized it's not always enough to have good habits. That's when I realized that I also needed to give up my bad habits — no matter how small they seemed. Dwelling on the past, feeling sorry for myself, and expecting immediate results, are just a few of the things that I had to give up if I wanted to be strong.

Then, a few years later when my father-in-law was diagnosed with terminal cancer, I wrote my list — 13 Things Mentally

Strong People Don't Do. Seeing all those things written down in one place really opened my eyes to the bad habits that could keep me stuck in a place of pain.

So while there wasn't a single epiphany, there were certainly "aha" moments along the way.

What were/are your day-to-day coping skills that keep you afloat?

I used the same skills I teach people in my psychotherapy practice. I used mindfulness skills to keep me from dwelling on the past or worrying too much about the future. I focused a lot on concrete problem-solving so I could get my life in order after the loss of my husband. And I spent a lot of time with my loved ones.

I also focused on self-care. I knew if I wasn't eating right or wasn't getting enough sleep, it would be impossible to manage my grief. I exercised every day and tried to take care of myself the best I could so I would have the strength to focus on healing.

In general, how have you managed to rebuild your life after your losses?

Well I knew it was best not to make any major decisions for at least a year after a sudden loss. So I stayed patient while I considered my future life changes. In the year after losing my husband I made some small changes, like selling our boat and buying a motorcycle, but I waited a long time before making any big changes.

I took my time to consider which goals I still wanted to pursue, and which dreams I wanted to let go. I developed some new interests and met new friends. And I held off on dating again for several years. But about four years later, I found love again and got remarried.

I've since moved to a new area and, over the last couple of years, my career has been kicked into overdrive. Writing about my experiences led to lots of new opportunities — including writing my book and being invited to lots of speaking engagements. My life is much different than it used to be, but I love what I do and I'm grateful for all that I have.

What advice would you offer someone going through loss, in the hope of coming out of the darkness able to re-engage with life in a meaningful way?

It's tempting to try to avoid the sadness and distress associated with grief — but if there's one thing I've learned, it's that you have to face your emotions head-on. Other people will try to cheer you up because they're uncomfortable with you being sad, but let yourself feel sad and angry and lonely.

Time doesn't heal anything. It's what you do with that time that matters. So it's important to use your time to heal — and part of healing means experiencing a wide variety of emotions. And don't be afraid to ask for help from friends, family, and professionals. Your connections with other people can make all the difference in the world.

Reference:
13 Things Mentally Strong People Don't Do by Amy Morin

૨♠

"PERMISSION TO BE HUMAN", as Tal Ben-Shahar, positive psychology researcher and teacher states, is a concept we all need to remember so that we can allow ourselves to feel the full gamut of emotions — including those yucky feelings from which we'd all rather escape. It's OK to feel and it's OK to feel bad. It's all part of the human deal of life — to go through it and feel the good along with the bad.

I spiraled down upon finding out my daughter had neurological deficits. I knew I had to seek help and save myself from the quicksand of grief that I was in over the loss of the normal baby I had expected. I spent a year in a therapist's office thrashing about in emotional pain — anger, bitterness, resentment,"why me?" — until eventually the dark clouds started to shift and the slightest rays of sunlight began to show themselves. Regurgitating all the negative feelings in me eventually cleaned me out and made room for some healing light to seep in. I was actually able to go to the park and be amongst other toddlers running around while mine was still having a hard time sitting up, without feeling the debilitating and prohibitive feelings of jealousy and resentment. My pain became more manageable.

And that's what we look and hope for —the pain to loosen its grip on us so that we can move around more freely. Confronting our feelings head-on gets them up and out so they don't take root in our system and slowly grow and spread their poisonous shoots. Working through our grief, as hard as it is, is what eventually gets us to the other side. And getting professional help along the way, when we feel overtaken and immobilized by the pain, can help in coping and getting through the difficult times.

Can you allow yourself to tolerate those bad and painful feelings? Can you sit with them and have them go through you? Will you reach out for help when they become too overwhelming?

Reference List

Ben-Shahar, Tal. 2012. *Choose the Life You Want: 101 Ways to Create Your Own Road to Happiness.* New York: The Experiment.

"A journey of a thousand miles begins with a single step."

Lao-Tzu

CHAPTER 14

Meditation — An Antidote to Anxiety

Meditation is a hot topic nowadays. With all the latest brain research being done showing the benefits of meditating, it's becoming much more prevalent in our society.

My next two interviewees use meditation as a means of managing anxiety and stress, as well as enhancing their overall wellbeing.

"To understand the immeasurable, the mind must be extraordinarily quiet, still."

Jiddu Krishnamurti

Taking Care of Our Mind

"Tame the voice in your head."

Dan Harris, journalist and ABC news co-anchor of Nightline and Good Morning America was the typical high-powered, high energy avoider and skeptic of any "woo-woo" meditation. Upon his return from reporting in the war zone areas of the world and having difficulty acclimating and managing his emotional lows, he learned how to "tame the voice in my head and reduce stress without losing my edge" by meditating. After suffering a panic attack on air, he began his journey into the self-help arena and found something that has made him *10% Happier* — the title of his best-selling memoir.

As a journalist having witnessed the horrors of war, what were some of your PTSD symptoms and how have you turned them into post traumatic growth?

I don't think I had PTSD. This isn't talked about much. But what messed me up in going to war zones was the adrenalin; I became addicted to the rush of it. That's not to say that I didn't witness things that people could describe as traumatic — I lost friends, I saw people in great distress, and I was shot at — but I just don't think that created my problem. I think it really was the adrenaline. In my book I describe it as journalistic heroin — the rush of being somewhere you're not supposed to be and, not only getting away with it, but getting on television. It's a high. When I came home the world seemed gray and uninteresting. I got depressed and I did a really dumb thing — I self-medicated, with coke and ecstasy and that led me to having a panic attack.

How did that lead to post traumatic growth? It was a winding road. It wasn't a direct line from panic attack to finding meditation. It was one event in the chain of events that got me to this place where I found something that I always thought was ridiculous, but it turns out to be very useful.

How have you taken control of your life beyond the standard treatment of therapy and medication?

Meditation, which is something I always reflexively rejected and thought was only for weirdos and gurus, turns out to have an enormous amount of science that strongly suggest it has a wide range of health benefits: everything from lower release of stress hormones to lower blood pressure, to higher functioning of the immune system, to literally rewiring key parts of the brain. When I learned about the science and when I learned that meditation did not involve wearing robes and lighting incense or chanting or joining any group or believing in anything, but that it's actually a very simple brain exercise, I decided to give it a shot. And I started five minutes a day, and that's what I recommend others do. I think it can have a significant impact. You can ignore all the self-help gurus who promise that you can solve all your problems through one simple technique. That is not what meditation will do for you. But it will give you a different relationship to those problems and that's transformational.

In terms of being a happy person, I think you use every arrow in the quiver, and that includes getting enough sleep, exercise, eating right and having good relationships in your life. All the studies show that relationships are often the most important variable. I happened to have married very well and we have really good friends; and I love my colleagues. There's another thing — gratitude is also very important. I think we have to pull every lever we can to make sure we're as happy as possible. For too long, meditation has been left out of the equation because it was thought to be either ridiculous or impossible. My argument is that we spend a lot of time and money taking care of our bodies, our cars and homes and pets, but we don't spend a lot of time taking care of the one filter through which we experience literally everything in our life, and that's our mind. And that's what meditation can help with.

As a type 'A' person, what has meditation been able to do for you?

I'm definitely type A, and I'm still type A and highly stressed even after starting meditation. I don't think meditation is designed to make you a lifeless blob. It does a couple of key things: it teaches you how to respond wisely instead of blindly reacting to the things in your life. So if somebody cuts you off on the road, rather than just automatically flying into a rage, you might be able to notice, "Oh I'm getting angry", and you can let it pass. That doesn't mean squashing it; it just means recognizing what's happening and making a decision — "Am I going to let my emotions yank me around or not?"

This doesn't work 100% of the time. There's a reason why I called the book, 10% Happier — some percentage of the time this tool will work. The other thing is, I still believe that strain, stress, striving, plotting, planning is all required if you're striving for excellence in any endeavor, be it professional, grand-parent-ing, volunteering, stay-at-home 'momming' (even though that's not a verb). All of those things require a lot of angst. What meditation can help you do is figure out when you cross the line between what I call 'constructive anguish' and useless rumina-tion. And so on the seventeenth time that I'm worrying about all the awful consequences of whether I'm going to make a flight, I've learned to ask myself, "Is it useful?" And often I'm able to cut myself off before I go down the rat hole of rumination and resentment. That means I spend less time miserable and also that I'm not taking out my stress as much on my wife.

What advice would you give others to bring in more happiness and wellbeing into their lives?

One of my regrets about the book is that I fear, inadvertently, I sent a message that meditation is for people who've got some sort of major problem — like I had a panic attack and therefore I meditate. In fact, meditation is for everybody. Specifically, it's good for well people; for high-achieving people who would never otherwise consider it. My argument is, you should give meditation a shot and all it takes is five minutes a day. It doesn't need to be another thing you add to your list of things to do that are stressing you out. Everybody has five minutes, even if you have 47 children and 17 part-time jobs. You've got five minutes, right when you wake up, right before you go to bed, when you pull the car into the driveway, before you go into the house; you can set your alarm on your phone and do five minutes. You can get instructions on the web. Just google mindful meditation and you'll find instructions that are incredibly simple. It also helps to go to a class and read books; but if you don't want to do that, you can learn the basics and go for it.

There are enough gurus for relationships and exercise and all that. I'm pro all of that but I'm largely focused on meditation.

Reference:
10% Happier by Dan Harris

૨૦

ONE OF THE BIGGEST BENEFITS IN MEDITATION is its ability to increase our resiliency by changing our reactive patterns to stress. We are more in control of how we respond to difficulties and stressors rather than simply reacting reflexively. We take notice of our discomfort, anger, frustration and then decide how to respond to it. It's a tool for stress management and for living a richly engaged life. We become more aware of ourselves and our surroundings, we appreciate more, feel more gratitude and wake up to life.

Richard Davidson, a renowned neuroscientist, is a leader in the field of neuroplasticity (the brain's ability to change its own structure). Diagnostic tools such as MRIs reveal that meditation effects changes in the brain structure.

We all need resiliency to deal with our challenges and set-backs. Now we know that we can 'grow' our resiliency and strengthen ourselves from the inside out. We can learn and implement new behaviors — such as meditation — with their physical and psychological benefits. In 1979, at the University of Massachusettes, Jon Kabat-Zinn created a program known as Mindfulness Based Stress Reduction or MBSR as a complementary form of medical treatment for various illnesses. By promoting relaxation and reducing anxiety it was shown that much pain and discomfort could be minimized. Five minutes a day is all we need to begin our journey towards greater well-being. And that's a doable action step!

Resource:

Guided meditation by Jon Kabat-Zinn (10 minutes)
https://www.youtube.com/watch?v=8HYLyuJZKno

"I can be changed by what happens to me. But I refuse to be reduced by it."

Maya Angelou

Bringing Calm to Life

"We can turn pain into understanding and growth."

"**I** haven't had a full-blown panic attack in a couple of years. Granted, my body is not always an ocean of tranquility. I still feel loneliness, fear, and what I call the black-and-blues — the sadness I finally allow myself to feel, the sadness that panic covered up for so many years."

Priscilla Warner is a noted writer, having co-authored a New York Times bestseller, *The Faith Club,* and a recent memoir, *Learning to Breathe.* She takes us on a fascinating journey as she seeks to find ways to heal from her years of suffering high anxiety and panic attacks.

Most, if not all of us, can relate to anxiety, but her condition was oftentimes very debilitating[1]. Priscilla shows us it's never too late to learn, grow and change or, as she says, "An old tiger can learn new tricks."

What personal qualities have helped you carry on and move in a positive direction?

My mother, a prolific artist, used to tell me, "People will disappoint you, but your work never will." The love I feel for my family and friends is the most powerful positive factor in my life. But often what sustains me most during tough times, propelling me forward, is my ability to create something from nothing, whether I'm writing or making art and jewelry.

Did you go through a period of self-pity? If so, what helped lift you out?

I didn't go through a period of self-pity, but I did feel shame when I suffered from panic attacks. I felt like I had a defective nervous system, which erupted at will, prohibiting me from functioning like a 'normal' person. What lifted me out of that shame was writing *Learning to Breathe,* because it sent me on a mission to heal that proved to be astonishingly effective.

Was there a specific moment, thought, or epiphany that helped to bring you to a better place mentally and psychologically, or did it evolve?

There was not one specific 'eureka' moment that turned me from an anxious person into a happy woman. I take life moment by moment now. My meditation practice helps me to note the happy, sad, anxious, boring, challenging instructive moments I experience, and be grateful as they string themselves together into one long life. The Thomas Wolfe quote I used for my high school yearbook is still surprisingly relevant! "Knowledge is finding out something for oneself with pain, with joy, with exultancy, with labor, and with all the little ticking, breathing moments of our lives."

What are your day-to-day coping skills that keep you afloat?

Meditation is a daily practice that helps me sustain a feeling of being grounded, at peace and in touch with my essence. I love knowing that all I need to do is observe my breath coming and going in order to feel empowered, healthy and happy. I also start my day with a short prayer of gratitude, which gets me off to the perfect start wherever else the day might take me.

What thoughts propel you forward?

The thought that propels me forward is, "This too shall pass."

What advice do you have for someone going through internal difficulties that greatly impact the quality of their life?

I've discovered that people can heal in ways they never thought possible. There are many resources out there to help make that possible. We can all turn pain into understanding and growth. We can choose the path we take through our suffering. That path will twist and turn in ways we can never expect. But if we put one foot in front of the other, and approach life one step at a time, we can move from a painful place to a productive one. We can accept sadness and feel grace. We can find teachers, therapists, techniques, experiences and resources that don't have to cost a fortune, but that can make a huge difference in our lives.

Learning To Breathe by Priscilla Warner

ॐ

PRACTICING MINDFULNESS KEEPS US IN THE PRESENT. Anxiety is future oriented. If we can stay focused in the present, a lot of that anticipatory worry can be minimized. Mindfulness is an awareness of the present — of ourselves in our surroundings and of our feelings. It's not looking in the rear-view mirror at our past and all that went wrong or what we didn't do, and it's not looking ahead at what may or may not happen; it's concentrating on the here and now. Multi-tasking is in direct opposition to mindfulness since we can't be mindful of any one thing while doing many at the same time. And that is a stressful condition. While multi-tasking was in vogue, we now need to focus more on doing one thing at a time. So when we eat, we need to just eat. Unlike what we all do — eat on the run, in the car, while working, and so on. Often we don't even know we've eaten and certainly can't appreciate the food we've ingested. We'd have a lot less digestive and weight issues if we only ate while eating.

Mindfulness meditation is the formal practice of quieting our overactive minds and becoming aware of when we're being pulled off into our thoughts again. Sitting quietly and watching our breath helps calm the nervous system and quiet the mind so that we're not all over the place. It's always interesting to me when someone who has difficulty focusing or sitting still, someone who may have attention deficit disorder (ADD), says meditation isn't for him because he can't sit still. That's like saying a person is too dirty to take a bath. It's even more needed for people who have difficulty attending to task, as a tool for increasing concentration and focusing ability.

Here's a quick visual to get rid of that constant nagging negative thought, at least for the moment: picture the thought as a leaf floating down a stream and watch it float away.

CHAPTER 15

Unlimited Parenting

To live a rich, wonderfully full and even exciting life, despite a permanent challenge, is no easy feat. It requires a choice — a conscious decision to integrate the adversity into one's life and not be defined by it. The next two interviewees both have children with cerebral palsy. They've each gone on to transform their challenge into service for others, and both live thriving lives.

What follows is a taste of their passion and enthusiasm, together with the obvious difficulties they face. And that's the key: 'together with'. The scale of life often tips downward for them, but it then comes back up enabling them to see and embrace beauty and richness once again as they continue opening up to a bigger life.

"My ability is stronger than my disability."

Theresa Sheridan

Unleashing the Limits of Dis-ability

"Disability is one aspect of our lives. It does not define it."

Laverne Bissky has incorporated a life-changing challenge, that of having a child with disabilities, into a goal and dream that takes her and her family to all corners of the earth. It's all about the 'A'-bilities without the 'Dis'. This incredible woman, together with her family, shows us how to not just live, but to flourish beyond the fate we've been given.

Ms. Bissky is a motivational speaker, writer and coach. She founded the charity, No Ordinary Journey Foundation, and is the author of the book, *Exceptional Parent Exceptional Life* (soon to be released).

What personal qualities have helped you move in such a positive direction?

A deep belief that the experience of having a severely disabled child could be a stepping stone to living a deeply fulfilled life. I guess you would call this optimism, but I think it goes so much deeper than that. Perhaps faith. It is a choice to see it this way.

In this belief was the seed that sprouted into our charity, No Ordinary Journey Foundation. It has been very gratifying to know that I have done the best I can for my own child, but it is even more gratifying to use what I have learned and lived

143

through to help those with children like mine in places like Vietnam. Their challenges are similar but their opportunities much fewer.

Did you go through a period of self-pity? If so, what helped lift you out?

After the first few months, my periods of self-pity have been intermittent and brief but deep. They usually resulted from asking questions that are unanswerable like, "Why Me?", and regretting things that cannot be changed, or worrying about the future. Doing something productive usually lifts me out of it.

Was there a specific moment, thought, or epiphany that helped guide you to a better place mentally and psychologically?

Shortly after Kasenya was diagnosed with cerebral palsy, I vowed that on my death bed I would be able to say that disability never held my family back. I didn't truly know what I was committing to at that time. And now I might word it differently: we would do the best we could and not put aside our hopes, goals and dreams because of the disability; that the disability would be one aspect of our lives. It would not define it. That simple commitment has kept me moving forward.

What were/are your day-to-day coping skills that keep you afloat?

For me coping is about balance: not static balance but dynamic balance because life is always in a state of flux. It's about knowing when to push hard and when to rest. When to fight and when to let go. When to use and when to conserve resources. When to work hard and when to have fun. Practicing mindfulness helps me to know when to shift between these. It's about paying attention to what is going on inside of you.

What thoughts propel you forward?

That every experience is an opportunity. I have noticed that when I am most sleep deprived, I am also most creative. When

I am most vulnerable, I am also the strongest. When I am most hurt, I am also the most loving. Our society is so afraid of negative experiences: failure, pain and death. And yet it is in these experiences that we have the greatest opportunities for growth. We can't live fully when we only embrace the "good" experiences in our lives. And so I see few things as good or bad; I see them all as opportunities.

In general, how have you managed to rebuild your life to such a flourishing degree?

At first it was about determination. We tried as many non-invasive therapies for Kasenya as time and money would permit. We wanted Kasenya to reach her full potential and we left few stones unturned.

Then it became about acceptance. Not that we stopped doing the therapies that worked, but acceptance allowed us to rise above the disability.

We didn't try to overcome the disability because that means fixing or changing it and results in a constant struggle. Rising above something means accepting it, which frees you to use it as a platform for greater things.

Finally, it was about setting priorities. When my son Devin set out the challenge of visiting all seven continents, we could have come up with all kinds of excuses. We have given up many luxuries in order to be able to travel to six continents (so far) as a family. Travel was the fertile ground from which the seed of our charitable work grew.

What advice can you offer others going through a difficult time/situation in the hope of living well?

It's going to be emotionally messy if you are really going to grow from a challenging experience. The sooner a person accepts that, the better off they will be. Embrace the experience. But have something to look forward to, something that will allow you to rise above it even if it is just knowing that you are becoming a stronger person. And go gently with yourself when you have setbacks.

I knew from the beginning that the challenge of parenting a child with a disability could be a catalyst for personal growth. But I thought it would be a straight-line process. I thought I would move steadily forward, sometimes quickly and sometimes slowly. It has actually been a circular process. I move forward and then I have a setback and circle back a bit. But each time I reach higher and I usually don't fall as far back.

Challenging experiences can be so powerful because they allow us to see things clearly. While others are bogged down with mental clutter, we begin to notice and focus on what is really important in life. Let go of trying to change things and just experience them. It's a choice.

❧

WE ARE THE CREATORS OF OUR LIFE. Things often happen to us, but we decide how we'll respond. We choose how we handle things. We need to realize that we do have choices, otherwise we're just going along for the ride, on auto-pilot, believing that everything happens to us and we are just the passengers getting driven to wherever. In other words, victims of our circumstances. We can "choose to choose" as Tal Ben Shahar says, and realize we have a lot more control than we think over ourselves and how we live our lives. Do we walk with our head down or with our head up, smiling at others as we pass them by? Do we immediately honk the guy in front of us when the light turns green or choose to wait it out, giving our patience a chance to flex its muscle? These are obviously little things. But it's the small things that create the 'feel' and texture of our lives.

A helpful technique is to reframe things so that we see them differently. For instance, rainy days can be disappointing if we have outdoor plans. However, they can also be seen as the time that flowers, plants and trees get their nourishment. We don't deny our disappointment, but we can deal with it better knowing there is another way to see it.

When my daughter got married, we were hoping for an outdoor ceremony. The florist even set up for it outside. And then came the rain. Of course we were all so disappointed. But (by making a choice) we weren't going to let that ruin a most meaningful and beautiful day. The indoor ceremony was done up in simple white drapery (since the flowers had all been set up outside) and it was an elegant chuppah indoors. And there was always that silver lining — women didn't complain their hair was frizzed out by the heat and humidity!

Resource:

http://www.noordinaryjourney.com/NoOrdinaryJourney/No_Ordinary_Journey.html

"There is no greater disability in society, than the inability to see a person as more."

Robert M. Hensel

Vision of Inclusion

"When you establish a vision, suddenly the negative doesn't feel like such a devastating blow."

Dan Habib is a photojournalist and producer of a documentary film, *Including Samuel.* The film portrays the Habib family's efforts to include their son, Samuel, in all aspects of their lives. Samuel has cerebral palsy.

Mr. Habib speaks candidly and openly about what it's like for him and his family to parent a child with a disability.

How do you overcome and carry on?

I don't think overcoming is the word I would use because I don't think you have to overcome in order to live with it, or manage it, or put it in a more positive context than just dealing with the negative. Sam has brought so many positive things to our life. I think it's made me a better person — a better parent, a better husband, a better friend. It's made me look at the world through an extremely different lens that has allowed me to see diversity in a whole new light; to see human rights in a completely different light. It has made me appreciate the value that each person brings to our society, regardless of their ability, economic condition or social status. I knew a lot of this before. My parents were civil rights activists and I was brought up with that in mind. But there's a difference between knowing it intellectually and experiencing it.

149

So for me, it's not about overcoming. It's about how you take something that is an enormous challenge and integrate it into your life so that you can continue to live a full, exciting and wonderful life, in addition to the challenges.

What are some of the challenges?

Having a child with a disability is very challenging, there's no doubt about it. It's challenging emotionally when you first learn about it and it completely turns your world upside down. It challenges your sense of what you thought the future would look like in a typical way for a typical family. It challenges your ability to cope with less sleep.

For us the biggest point of adversity has probably been the fear; coping with the fear of Samuel's health — the fact that he does have an underlying health condition. I joke — if it was just cerebral palsy that would be easy. But he has an underlying mitochondrial disorder which makes his health much more fragile. So when he gets sick, he gets really sick. When he gets a stomach bug, he usually ends up in the hospital. When he gets the flu, it can be life-threatening. So there's a lot more to it than just a physical disability.

Someone will ask me, "How is Samuel doing?" And I say there are two answers to that question. The first answer is, he's doing theatre, he's starring in Fiddler on the Roof, he's playing baseball, he's following the Red Sox, he's got lots of friends over, he's started karate, he's doing skiing. All true.

The other answer is, he's having these uncontrollable movements, he's on 15 different kinds of medicines, and he's fatigued easily. We're also waiting on some blood work that may give us new information on his disorder.

You have to take both those answers.

It seems like you've created a lot of good as an outgrowth of the negative. Can you speak to that?

I think we have. I think the first thing is to realize that the negative is not as negative as you think. And that's really about creating a vision for your child and your family. A very strong vision. Our vision came out of our Leadership Series at the University of New Hampshire, where we had incredible role models from all over the country showing us what's possible: that Samuel can have an incredibly full and happy life; he can have rich relationships; he can go to college and have a great profession. That's all possible. I think when you establish that vision, suddenly the negative doesn't feel like such a devastating blow. It's critical to have that vision. That gives you energy to do some things you wouldn't feel the energy to do otherwise.

For me that leadership series I took through the Institute on Disability, which is where I work now, gave me the vision for the film; for taking my background as a documentarian and finding a way to tell a story of what it's like to be a parent of a child with a disability, and use that experience to hopefully benefit other people; and change our school system and community.

How do you continue to maintain a strong and positive demeanor?

It is truly from Samuel. Samuel is a kid that has been through more medically than I've ever gone through in my whole life. He's had more blood work, CAT scans, MRI's, serious illnesses, than most of us have in a lifetime. And still he wakes up every day with a smile and an optimistic outlook on the world, and kindness and compassion and a great sense of humor. That has just given me such incredible strength. He is definitely a role model for me. And he's definitely one of the strongest people I've ever met in my life. Obviously I don't mean that in a physical sense, but in strength of character and emotion and persistence. His persistence is incredible.

Staying strong as a family unit and specifically as a couple has been important. We work hard to even things out, to create more of a balance in how we share the many responsibilities of Samuel's health and educational concerns.

I respond by channeling a lot of my energies into my work. It's been healthy for me but also tricky. At first when I was working on *Including Samuel,* I almost used the film as a place to get lost, away from the daily stresses and realities and fears. My wife called it 'Planet Dan'. There were times when I was making the film, that my head was so into the film that I wasn't as connected to our family and to her as I should've been.

Was there a specific moment, thought, or epiphany that helped guide you to a better place mentally/psychologically?

We didn't realize he had a disability at birth. It was a gradual process. He was not hitting the developmental milestones. It unfolded over a period of time. But there was one moment I think that was the lowest point in my life, when one of his neurologists called, who we no longer work with for self-evident reasons, who said, "I think he has mitochondrial disorder." We didn't know what that meant so we did what parents do now — went on google. It said, 'usually fatal'. And that was when I felt "Anything short of this I can handle." Once you or a loved one has had a near-death experience — or in this case, a near-death diagnosis — it changes your perspective on everything. Getting Samuel up and changed and dressed and ready, doesn't seem so bad when you think, I'm happy for this moment, this day.

What qualities within you help you carry on?

I am a very optimistic person by nature. That helps. It's good to be optimistic, but you can't let that create denial of some of the challenging realities. The problem is if you're only optimistic and can't acknowledge some of the fears or difficulties, your partner feels very alone, and so do the other kids. We realized that in terms of Isaiah. If we weren't honest with him about our fears and stresses, he would've picked those up. Kids have incredible radar. And he might then feel all alone in feeling those fears.

There's another big component and that is my own foundation; my foundation of what I was given as a child through my family. I had a very stable, loving and supportive family life. I had that love and support where I felt good about myself. I think that gives you energy when you've been nurtured. And that gives you a positive outlook on life. You have to tap into that every day to manage these challenges.

Sometimes I feel that everything in my life kind of prepared me for this moment. Some are resources I was given by other people — by Betsy (my wife), by my parents and by the experience of raising Isaiah for three years before having Samuel.

What keeps you going?

We learned to ask for help. And we learned to accept help. We realized we needed it. Samuel needs 100% attention most of the time. He needs someone a few steps away.

Betsy and I make sure we carve out time for ourselves. We've made it a priority to take care of our relationship. And also to make sure we have lots of time with Isaiah and with the family as a whole.

We have a very strong local community in Concord, New Hampshire. We are amazed at the openness and support we have received for including Samuel in school and recreational activities. That's why it makes me sad, and at times horrified, to hear about the obstacles some families face to include their child with disabilities in the most simple, basic ways. So much of what could be draining for people when you have to fight those fights every day, is not draining for us. That's a huge factor. It's so critical.

What pearls of advice do you have?

The vision — it helps sustain you. And don't compromise because of the disability.

Communication — make time to speak openly and honestly. Try not to let that challenge always dominate the conversations.

Ask for help — learn to be comfortable asking. There are people who want to be there for you. You can't sit back and hope people respond. Let people know how they can be helpful.

I hope this is the greatest challenge we ever face. I hope I've already faced the hardest part of it. In some ways my life is richer and happier than it would've been otherwise. I appreciate every moment.

᠕᠕

THEN THERE'S STILL THE REST OF THE FAMILY. Tending to the needs and time-consuming care of the child with the disability as well as the other family members is a huge and stressful juggling act. But it's one we can't ignore. And no matter how hard we try, the other children and spouse may still get short-changed or certainly feel that way. We must at least be aware of this so we can do our best to give them their due attention and build in opportunities for togetherness.

It's important to be open about our feelings with one another so nobody feels alone with their 'bad' emotions. It's a big burden to feel like we have to put on a good strong front for others. We need to give ourselves permission to be human — to allow for those tough emotions as well as the easier and better ones.

When I was living up at the rehab hospital during the weekdays, I made it my business to do something fun with my younger daughter, Penina, on Sundays. The ICU doctor had given me the best advice — "Don't forget about your other kids; they're going through this too. And they need some normalcy in their lives." I would sit on Penina's bed at night and express how hard it must be for her being at home without me all week while still trying to focus on school. I was giving her permission to 'let it out' to me but she kept a tight lid on it, maybe as a protective shield for herself and/or so as not to feel like she was burdening me further with her 'stuff'. I hope that although she didn't articulate her pain and hardship, hearing me acknowledge it provided some sense of comfort.

Just everyday living with a child with disabilities requires lots of extra care. Two to three times a week I was taking Nava to her different therapies. Penina, as a child, was always 'shlepping' along. I couldn't help that, but I realized I could make something positive out of it, make it somewhat enjoyable for her. And so I'd drop Nava off and we'd go to the park, play in the snow, jump in the autumn leaves, read books in the office, or go for ice cream. It became our one-on-one special time for that hour. That was probably more than she would've gotten at home on any given day. We must create that silver lining for the others in the family. For me, I had a choice how to spend that hour waiting for Nava and, to this day, Penina remembers those times fondly and often refers back to our making big piles of leaves and jumping in them together.

Resource:

http://www.includingsamuel.com/home.aspx

"Hardships often prepare ordinary people for an extraordinary destiny."

C.S. Lewis

CHAPTER 16

Fighting the Perpetrator by Living Well

"Everyone has their own schedule of healing."

Natasha Alexenko is a woman who epitomizes the concept of taking lemons and making lemonade. She has taken her personal trauma and turned it into the meaningful endeavor of helping others in a similar situation.

Ms. Alexenko is a survivor of sexual assault. A newcomer to New York, she was just 20 years old when she was raped in the stairwell of her Manhattan apartment building. It took 16 years for her to witness justice being served, when the perpetrator was finally found and jailed.

Her rape kit, which includes the specimens collected during a sexual assault forensic exam, sat on a shelf in a police storage facility for more than ten years. Because of this she began an organization known as *Natasha's Justice Project* whose goal is to ensure these rape kits of evidence get tested and investigated more quickly. Currently, an estimated 180,000 such kits nationwide are sitting on shelves untested. Ms. Alexenko is hoping to remediate this backlog crisis.

This story is featured in an HBO documentary called 'Sex Crimes Unit.'

What personal qualities helped you carry on and move in a positive direction?

I'm grateful to have a network of family and friends supporting me from the beginning and on to today.

The thing that was helpful to me was that I asked for help. I think if you have a support system in place rather than handling it on your own you should be able to say, "I really need help with this, I'm having difficulty." You just have to ask — especially in a case where not everyone knows what you're going through. They may not be able to approach you for help. You have to find it in yourself to lower your barriers and say, "I'm still OK if I ask for help; it doesn't speak to my strength or weakness." That's actually a good quality to have — to be able to recognize when there's something you cannot handle on your own and know the appropriate people to turn to for help.

I didn't know anyone in my building and after this occurred I knew everyone in my building and I went to everyone's house for dinner at some point. Part of it was allowing myself to be vulnerable and letting people take care of me.

Did you go through a period of self-pity and if so what helped you come out of it?

Absolutely, I felt sorry for myself for a long time. And then I eventually started to ask myself, "What am I thankful for out of this situation?" I started going through things I was very grateful for: first of all, that I'm alive. That was the first step; what could've happened and that didn't, and then my gratitude in the present tense — the people, my job, my dog. Of course it's easier to find the negatives than the positives, but to find those positives and hold onto them and through repetition — everyday waking up and saying, "I love my family, I love my friends, I love my dog." And I'm so grateful to have them there.

Was there a specific moment or epiphany that helped guide you to this better place psychologically? Or did it evolve?

I think it evolved, and there were many epiphanies. I remember the first time I laughed; it was a true belly laugh. It made me realize I hadn't been laughing before.

The first time I wasn't afraid to go out anymore was big; little triumphs that got me through everything.

What in general are your day-to-day coping skills that keep you afloat?

One is if I'm not OK, if I'm upset or have a bad day, to allow myself that; no pressure. Tonight it's OK to just watch TV and not worry that there are dishes in the sink. Learning to not be so hard on myself and give myself an opportunity to be sad or bored. You don't always have to be productive. You're biggest responsibility is to yourself and making sure you're OK. If you are not feeling well emotionally or mentally, you should treat yourself almost like you're ill. If you had a cold you wouldn't necessarily mop your floors or do your laundry. You're allowed to take a moment to smell the roses and not be hard on yourself.

What thoughts propel you forward?

Rewarding myself and allowing myself to be happy. It feels good to go out and have a great time; those sorts of normal experiences help heal and they helped me feel like I wasn't wearing a scarlet letter. Allowing myself to do what feels good and right.

We're constantly evolving, testing things out and seeing where we are in life. And being inspired by things around us. Allow for this.

It's very important to forgive. I haven't forgotten but I have forgiven.

What does it mean to forgive such a crime?

It is the most empowering thing to be able to forgive someone who has done something like this to you. It takes his power away. It makes you like yourself. It's freeing. Being angry traps you. When you're able to forgive and move on, it frees you. I had years of therapy and years of feeling angry. Eventually your mind has to go somewhere after that. You can't stay angry and continue to function. It was almost a survival instinct to forgive, to work through that process. You start to learn to put that energy toward other things; you change the focus.

I couldn't fight this guy physically; he had a gun. But how I can fight him and win is by continuing on with my life and not let what he did to me affect me. And now I'm going to take what happened to me and help other people. Now I'm fighting even harder. He's already lost the battle.

What advice would you give to someone?

Everyone has their own schedule of healing.

Recognize you're not alone.

Talk about it.

Find who you truly are.

࿏

WHEN WE'RE IN THE THROES OF AN AWFUL SITUATION, to be able to stop and think of something to be grateful for is a huge challenge; to find that 'at least', as I like to call it.

When my daughter, Nava, was in the ICU in an induced coma on a respirator, I would say to myself, "At least she's in a great hospital with fabulous doctors." What if that weren't the case? There had been no time to select the top place; she was admitted there straight from the emergency room. When my younger daughter had to be at home 24/7 with her stepdad, I said, "At least she has a good relationship with him." If she hadn't, it would've been more problematic. Holding on to the pieces of gratitude can keep us afloat when we feel we're sinking.

Anger, though, is a normal and natural response to a horrible situation which feels so unfair and unjust. It can propel us towards doing what we need to do. But living in a state of anger, or constantly coming back to it, is toxic to our body and mind.

It can grow like a cancer and overtake us so that we become bitter, resentful and miserable. And what a lousy existence that is. Working it through by giving voice and healthy expression to it eventually helps diffuse it. It loses some of its hold on us. But we have to be willing to confront it and tackle it head-on. The alternative is to bury it inside and then, like a tube of toothpaste, it starts to ooze out from the holes and makes a mess. It comes out in all the wrong times and places. It can also manifest itself in addictive and unhealthy behaviors.

We have to go through to come through.

When I found out Nava had disabilities, I raged in a therapist's office for a year until I no longer felt choked by my grief. The strangulating grip gave way, which eventually allowed some positive feelings to surface. I began to smile, to laugh, and actually started feeling pride and joy when Nava worked hard and attained some milestones, however late they were. To see her pull herself up to a standing position — finally at the age of two and a half — brought me to tears.

Forgiveness is a very difficult concept and one that I cannot, in all honesty, write much about. I understand it intellectually, but have no clue what it means in practice — to be able to let an injustice go and live free. I can say that living well after any kind of perpetrated tragedy is the best form of revenge. It puts the ball back in our court and takes away the perpetrator's power over us. It's certainly not an easy place to come to. The fight begins with oneself. As we see here though, it is possible.

Resources:

Natasha's Justice Project — http://natashasjusticeproject.org/

RAINN — Rape, Abuse and Incest National Network — https://rainn.org/

*"Dogs have a way
of finding the people
who need them, filling an
emptiness we don't
even know
we have."*

Thom Jones

CHAPTER 17

"Live, Love, Laugh"
With Service Dogs

*"I choose to define myself not by what I must over-
come, but by what I have the strength to become."*

 Leigh Brill is a writer, motivational speaker, counselor and advocate for people with disabilities. I read an excerpt from her book, *A Dog Named Slugger*, in Ability Magazine, and was immediately drawn in. Ms. Brill, who has cerebral palsy, has spent more than 10 years "in the company of service dogs".

For Ms. Brill, having congenital cerebral palsy means, "I cannot depend on my body to do what I want it to do." She has difficulty with muscle coordination and movement and lives in constant pain. Things like picking up a dropped hairbrush or stepping into the shower can be frustrating and difficult.

What qualities have helped you carry on and move in a positive direction?

I've been called stubborn at times, but I have found that my determination has served me well over many years. I also like to think beyond the obvious limits in life. That's one reason I love working with service dogs — our partnerships have helped me grasp the potential and power of creative problem solving. I often depend on my sense of humor to keep a good perspective. My dogs help with that too.

I've also found personal strength in recognizing that my life, my experience, is part of a bigger picture. My goal is to make the most of what I've been given while at the same time be part of a goodness far greater than me.

Did you/do you go through periods of self-pity? What helped lift you out so you could see beyond it?

I feel the saddest about my situation when I look back at what I had to endure as a child. I have an easier time dealing with more current issues because I have the benefit of a more mature perspective. The best way I have found to deal with the sadness I feel about some of my past struggles is to make sure I use the gifts I have in my life now and try to make a difference for other young people who may be going through some of the same struggles I faced years ago. That brings healing to other people and to me at the same time.

What thoughts propel you forward?

I have many blessings in my life. Acknowledging them and expressing thanks for them is important to me. That's where I find strength to move forward, even if that means taking slow baby steps.

My service dogs also help me move forward, both literally and figuratively. In addition to the mobility assistance they provide, they have each shared valuable wisdom.

Slugger taught me that even the greatest challenges in life can hold the promise of something good. Kenda inspires me to be mindful of the question: "What will I do with the gifts I have been given?" And the newest canine member of our family, Pato, proclaims, "Live, love, laugh!" in everything he does. With such lessons, I can't help but move forward!

What are your day-to-day coping skills that keep you going strong?

I always try to remind myself not to over-complicate or worry too much about day-to-day ups and downs. There is peace in taking life as it comes. I've also found that pacing is good — if I stay in touch with my physical, emotional and spiritual self, I'm better able to determine the best way to spend my days.

I'm fortunate to be surrounded by loved ones who understand this; and in fact my loved ones are a vital part of my coping skill set. I have discovered that life is much more positive and rewarding when I make a point of surrounding myself with the people and things I love.

Speak to your phrase of "making possibilities out of challenges".

The question I often ask myself is: What will I do with what I have been given? This applies to challenges as well as victories. Personally, I wanted — I needed — to give some meaning and purpose to my congenital disability. And writing A Dog Named Slugger allowed me to do that. I guess I am too stubborn to let the hard aspects of cerebral palsy have the 'last word'. I choose to define myself not by what I must overcome, but by what I have the strength to Become. I also believe that every part of life offers the promise of something good; and making possibilities out of challenges means reaching for that goodness, no matter what.

I avoid using outdated descriptions such as: deformed, crippled, handicapped, afflicted, wheelchair-bound, a CP case, stricken with a disability, when referring to myself or someone who lives with a disability. To me, such labels perpetuate negative stereotypes. They diminish the varied gifts and talents that all individuals — including those of us living with physical challenges — can offer. I consider my cerebral palsy something I have; it is not who I am.

What advice would you offer someone going through a tough time in life?

When facing a challenge, here are the points I try to keep in mind:

Breathe.

Stay in touch with yourself and who you are; do things that keep you grounded.

Remember that life holds a bigger picture than what is right in front of your eyes in this particular moment.

Find people and causes with whom you can connect and stay in touch.

When you need help, ask for it. When you can give help, offer it.

A Dog Named Slugger by Leigh Brill

&

MAKING SOMETHING BIGGER OUT OF SOMETHING that appears to be limiting broadens our perspective and helps us look for those opportunities that can be discovered in the murky waters of adversity. It all starts with our mindset. Potential lies waiting within us to be brought forth even in the throes of the most difficult challenges.

Do you realize you can become more than what your disability or circumstance seems to dictate? Do you believe it? There's always more 'becoming' we can do.

On my Top Ten list of meaningful things I've done is having raised a service dog. I started out applying for one for my daughter, Nava, but quickly decided against it when I learned that it would be trained to do lots of wonderfully amazing things, thereby fostering dependence on a dog. I wasn't looking to encourage more couch-potato lethargy as the dog would get the remote, turn on and off lights, even open the refrigerator. And so my husband and I decided we'd flip it and we'd become the puppy raisers for someone else with disabilities. Unlike with children, the dog came with an instruction manual that we followed to a T to maximize the chances that he'd pass his tests and qualify to become a service dog. After 19 months, our beautifully sleek and trim Yael, went back to his home agency to undergo tests and more advanced training. After successfully passing, he qualified to be paired up with someone waiting for a companion dog. He went through training with his potential new owner and then attended a graduation ceremony. We walked him up onstage (along with many other graduating dogs) and handed him over to his new family — a little boy with cerebral palsy, and his parents and brother. Yael was to now live out his life's mission, by assisting a child to maximize and enrich his life. My heart soared with pride, joy and tremendous satisfaction. And to think, in the time we had him he only ate one shoe — my mother's, from whom he {correctly} smelled disdain.

Resource:

Canine Companions for Independence (CCI): www.cci.org

"Life takes you to unexpected places. Love brings you home."

Unknown

CHAPTER 18

A Monkey's Helping Hand

"You have to go up one step at a time to get out of that vortex; otherwise it will suck you in."

When tragedy strikes, it's natural to feel like a victim of circumstance. It's only with time and work that we can move from a victim mentality to 'survivor' and eventually 'thriver'. Ned Sullivan has been able to dig deep and reclaim his positivity and humor to help him cope and live on with his dramatic life change.

Eight years ago he was in a near fatal car accident that left him paralyzed. He has been rebuilding his life with the incredible help of a capuchin monkey named Kasey. Together they work and play. "I'm happy to help out any way I can. I think I have a lot to offer people."

How does Kasey help make your life better?

I've had Kasey for about seven years. I'm thirty now. I was injured at the age of twenty-two. When I was twenty-three, Helping Hands: Monkey Helpers for the Disabled donated Kasey to us. That was after an extensive application and after a year being home. I was in the hospital for a year and I was home for a year before I got Kasey. It had been two years where I had been in a place where there was a lot of medication, I was constantly confused. I had a bad injury — quadriplegic. Moving forward we decided to get a monkey to inject some positivity into my life. At the time my comprehension was only so-so. I've come a long way since then.

What does Kasey do for you day-to-day?

When I got her I couldn't do much in terms of moving my muscles. She did practical things at that time. She knew I couldn't do things for myself. She's very smart like that and is able to see who's in the room, who's helping Ned, what's my job, what's my reward. With such a strong animal/human bond, they often don't need a reward. They do it out of love. In the beginning, you needed to ask her. Now, it's almost like she's able to read my mind. If I'm exiting or entering a room, she flips on and off the lights. She opens the door. If I drop my magazine, she gets it for me. But this is almost seven years now. They were trained to remove or fetch from a laser light. I point to a towel on the ground and she'll stop what she's doing and get the towel. She knows what that red light reflecting on something means for her.

What has given you the strength to move on and be so positive?

My attitude. If you have the right attitude, you can conquer anything. I turn to different things to help reshape my attitude. If I'm having a downer day, I try to keep positive because I know it will carry out into what I do. I learned this way before my injury. After a certain amount of time I can regroup within myself. That's not to say Kasey is not a huge help because she is. Her presence is a lift of positive energy.

I like to look at it as one day at a time. I try to build day by day and make a positive action that will help me looking forward.

What advice can you give people going through difficult times?

I would say to try to do your best. Don't ever become a victim. It's really low. I came across a quote that I put away in a file:

> *"Things turn out best for the people who make the best of the way things turn out." John Wooden*

It all starts with attitude. If you remain positive you will find it easier to not continuously fall into the trap of being a victim. I was lucky enough to enter the situation where I had this positivity inside me.

Having a strong support system, whether you were injured or going through a drug addiction or just down makes a huge difference. And it will continue to make an enormous difference going forward.

Being able to make a difference in other's lives is extremely worthwhile. When feeling down, helping people is always a way to help yourself.

Ellen Rogers, Ned's mom, is the author of the book, *Kasey to the Rescue.*

"I'm always looking for new ways for him to be challenged and to grab onto things that he can get excited about."

What personal qualities have helped you carry on and move in a positive direction?

Let's start with the fact that Ned didn't die. That's how I begin with anything. This is the most wonderful part even though he was so badly injured. As long as he stayed alive, we were making some progress.

I was very lucky because I had been in business for a long time. I had been a marketing executive for 25 years at many large high-tech and start-up successful companies. I had established a lot of business skills. I realized as I was facing each challenge with Ned that much of my ability to move him forward with the insurance, doctors, treatment and all that, came from my good and fine-tuned problem solving, resourcefulness and ability to manage complex tasks that were from my business world. Was I born that way? I don't know. But these skills were very important in business as they got me to where I was, and I realized that those were the key elements of how I was able to keep going with Ned.

Most people when confronted with a crisis don't necessarily have business experience. All of these things — creative problem-solving, resourcefulness, a keen ability to manage complex tasks — are within each one of us. You have to believe that you can do these things. When you're overcome with sadness and fear and you don't know what you're going to do because your loved one is so badly hurt or has cancer, your vision and ability to harness your own internal capabilities are severely compromised as well. Your vision is clouded. You can't see opportunities. It's almost impossible when you're so dragged down into the horror of whatever you're doing to be able to see any hope or opportunity. Opportunity is what you have to be resourceful with and you have to be creative to solve problems and be able to grab onto hope. You may not even realize the opportunities at the moment.

I believe that every one of us has these capabilities. You have to dig deep and you have to believe somewhere in your heart, in your soul, that you do have them. Because if you don't believe that you do, then you can't access them. Whenever I talk to groups I say the same thing. I'm not the lone ranger here. Every single person in the audience has his own personal challenge — business, personal, family. You don't just lie on the ground and roll over. You pick yourself up because, at the end of the day, you have to face it. Some people do it with greater difficulty than others. People have to get up and put one foot in front of the other. Especially if you're a single parent like I am.

What thoughts and strategies kept you going?

In my marketing days, we had to help our sales forces with what we called 'overcoming the no'. We had to come up with how to 'overcome the no' in sales. It was not a whole lot different with Ned than when I would hear, "No we can't do that" or a 'no' from the insurance company or case manager.

I learned to keep moving forward. A famous motto of one of my CEOs was 'to ask permission is to seek denial'. He was a very bold guy and we were all encouraged to be risk takers and to be bold and move forward even at some amount of peril because to ask permission would be to seek denial. Whether it was needing to use the cell phone when it said 'No cell phone' or needing to push the case managers more when they said "no" to Ned having another two weeks of therapy, I just kept going.

Did you go through a period of self-pity?

I have my 'woe is me, wow this is really awful', but I have as few moments as I can of that because it's not productive. And then I go, "OK I can do it."

It's so useless to do self-pity because there's no positive outcome to it. We're a family of non-victim people. At the end of the day, there's me and me and me. I've got to earn the money, pay the bills, take care of Ned and make sure he's going to be taken care of in the long run, and I have four other children and two grandchildren now. I have to do the best to manage things so we can all have the best possible opportunities. This is my job. It keeps me focused.

You've unfortunately had so many losses to deal with.

I have and that's point number two after the business stuff. I've unfortunately had a lot of experiences with family tragedies. It's helped me (as well as my children) in navigating the medical and hospital world.

My feeling at the end of the day is what else is there to do but to try to be positive. I find being negative and worrying zaps me; it takes away energy from doing something positive. If I'm wringing my hands, and believe me I've done my share, and when I'm sad, I let myself be really sad and allow that, but I can't let it consume me. It's hard to get out of that. It becomes a vicious cycle. You become more and more depressed. I'm not saying that everybody should be able to snap their fingers and get out of it. A psychiatrist working with my daughter after my divorce (when she was about eight) drew a picture of a spiral. My daughter had been describing to him what it felt like — that she was being pulled down into it. He then drew a staircase and told her she can climb up the stairs one at a time to get out.

I have used this visual a million times. You have to go up one step at a time to get out of that vortex; otherwise it will suck you in.

How about a little monkey business?

The monkey, Kasey — we haven't even talked about her. Her devotion, intelligence and loyalty are astounding. As a result of the relationship, I've become very involved with the organization that trains them, Helping Hands: Monkey Helpers for the Disabled. It is like having another child, a three-year-old. But she brings me a lot of personal enjoyment. She makes me laugh. We've had her almost seven years now.

What advice can you offer people going through difficult challenges?

Resiliency is a core trait. It's there. All of us have it. It's part of who we are as human beings. Finding it, nurturing it, fanning it and utilizing it to your advantage is a lot harder. As I said earlier, what choice do we have? We look at the situation and say, "This is what needs to be done and I will find a way." Then we can go back to that stairway. It's going to be really hard but let me take the first step out of this trap and go up the next one, knowing you're going to tumble. I think people confronting long cancer deaths — it's a big challenge because the end doesn't look good. Trying to keep yourself buoyant during a long haul is very hard. If you're not going to do it for yourself, you do it for the ones you love, you help them.

Kasey to the Rescue by Ellen Rogers

છે

SOME OF US SEEM TO BE BORN WITH MORE 'OOMPH' than others; predisposed towards a more positive life-long attitude. We look at these people and think, "I could never do that or be like that, or handle that." And then there are people who seemingly can't do it — whatever 'can't' means. They fall into a depression, feel like they can't go on, fall apart and can't manage. But that doesn't mean they 'can't'. It simply means they haven't discovered their hidden abilities and reservoir of strengths. It means they've been knocked down and haven't grabbed onto that lifeline, yet. It means the cloud of darkness is so thick and enveloping that they haven't been able to notice even the smallest bit of light coming through.

When we're going through the worst situations, we don't have the energy to grow our attitudinal muscle and our strength and resilience. It's enough to just stay afloat and not drown in sorrow. But often times we surprise ourselves and see that we have more strength and ability than we thought. When put to the test, many rise. But if we can't pick our heads up, that's OK too, for a bit, while we lick our wounds. We need to remember to give ourselves 'permission to be human'.

When I look back I'm amazed that I was able to get through the year of Nava's medical crisis like I did. I've decided that's why we can't look into a looking glass and see the future. If we knew what was ahead, we might quit right from the get-go. I guess nature, the universe, God, knows that if we know too much in advance we'll close up shop and say "I can't do this." And so we plow forward, hard and painful as it is because our natural tendency is to lean into survival.

If I had known in advance that Nava would be on a ventilator for three months, and then nine more in a rehab hospital, I would've thought to myself that there's no way I'd be able to live through that. But since we often don't know what we're up against, we almost mindlessly put one foot in front of the other and keep on going. What's the alternative? Curling up in a ball under the covers and camping out there? Yes, we can do that for a while. But eventually we get back out there doing what we need to do.

I'm a hiker. If I were to keep looking up and seeing how far away I was from my destination, I'd probably be calling it quits many times throughout the hike, saying, "I can't do this." But by focusing on each step I eventually get to that target point. When we string along each little step we see how far we've gotten, giving us the hope and motivation to continue on.

Painful emotions can hinder us from taking action, even paralyze us. And yet oftentimes, we must push through them and take action through the lousy feeling, and climb toward that hint of sunlight. We need to believe that we have the inner resources to carry us, despite and through the deep, painful hole in our heart.

What are some of your strengths? Do take the VIA character strength survey listed in the resources below and start to utilize your top five if they are in alignment with how you see yourself. Become aware of them and intentionally bring them forth. Doing this will enrich your life and help you cope. One of my top strengths is being able to appreciate beauty and excellence. I know that putting myself out in nature and surrounding myself with its beauty is very soothing and healing for me. I actually discovered hiking and my love of nature when Nava was in the rehab hospital. Someone had told me about a local hiking group so I decided to give it a shot since it was fairly close by. It took me out of the sick world and into something expansive and peaceful where I was enveloped in beauty. I grew to love these weekly hikes so much so that it's become a part of my life ever since. For my big '5-0' birthday, two years after Nava came home and was re-engaged in her life, my husband and I took our first big hiking trip to the Swiss Alps. It represented a miraculous climb of healing and recovery for my daughter and a deep appreciation for the mysteries and awesomeness of life as I was forging ahead in my own second lease on life.

Resources:

Organization: http://www.monkeyhelpers.org/

Ned and Kasey: https://www.youtube.com/watch?v=iGdHjSyry-A&feature=youtu.be

VIA Survey: http://www.viacharacter.org/www/The-Survey

CHAPTER 19

Growth From the Inside Out

"Ultimately our limitations really are self-imposed."

"If *we keep staring at the closed doors, we won't see the open windows."*

Julie Genovese is a writer and inspirational speaker. Her memoir, *Nothing Short of Joy,* is truly nothing short of uplifting and motivating. She suffers from a type of dwarfism which has left both physical and emotional scars. Her physical difficulties involve limited flexibility due to the reconstruction of her knees and hips, joint pain due to arthritis, and pain with limited movement in her shoulder. These all affect her daily life and oftentimes interfere with her painting and writing — the work she loves.

As you will see here, she transcends her pain and challenges by focusing on her spiritual and inner work.

What personal qualities have helped you carry on and move in a positive direction?

My desire for joy. I grew up believing it wasn't possible because I was born with SED, a type of dwarfism associated with degenerative arthritis. I felt I had several strikes against me. What kept me moving me forward was this hope that maybe I was wrong. I think deep down our soul does know that we are in fact all love, all joy. What also kept me going was my connection to my spirit. It felt small for a while because I was so immersed in challenges and difficulties.

I didn't realize I had a choice of how to see my challenges. When I turned it around to see those challenges as adventures or as mountains to climb so that I could see a fantastic view, my attitude changed; that shift in perspective would change all of it. I realized I did have more of this inner divine power than I had realized in the past.

It's a universal quality that keeps us moving forward. It's that desire to be our own truth, to be our whole self. We are all born into these different handicaps, visible or invisible, and they are the catalyst to wake us up and remind us that we came here for growth and awareness.

Our hardship and struggles are that springboard to appreciate what we can have here if we look at it differently, or if we experience it with new senses — like jumping into a pool after a horribly hot day is ten times better than jumping into a pool every day when you've never really gotten hot. As humans we have these catalysts to keep prodding us forward and to keep remembering there's a greater and more beautiful truth than maybe what we're living.

Did you go through a period of self-pity? If so, what helped lift you out?

Oh my goodness, yes — and I still have these times. I wouldn't have labeled it as self-pity as a youngster because I thought life was against me. I thought I was born either an accident or a punishment or some kind of genetic mutation, and therefore others pitied me, and I should as well. I felt I had no choice, and of course that's never true. In our family, as in many families, we didn't talk about our negative emotions — sadness, anger. We just didn't bring them up. Although my mom was open to that — she used to say it's good to cry — my dad wasn't. I think we all wanted to honor my parents by not showing them that there was anything wrong with us. We wanted to only show the positive side. It was this unspoken rule that you keep smiling through the pain and let it roll off your shoulders. I found myself in that pity party because I had nowhere else to direct the pain.

Pity leads to depression because if there's no place for that kind of voltage, which we all have known and felt, if there's no place to express it, then it goes inside and starts to detonate. There are days when my old habits about myself come up and I wonder, 'am I enough, am I doing enough, am I giving enough?'

I considered myself "less than" the rest of the population for so many years. I still have that habit, but fortunately it lasts for a few hours or a day.

Emotions need expression; they don't need judgement. Once they're expressed they move, transform and change.

But I held them in. I repressed them. I shoved them under the bed. I did whatever I could so no one would see my humanness. Since my body was different and it was this billboard of negative attraction, I thought I certainly couldn't show any other vulnerability. I had no idea that to express these vulnerabilities that we all have, actually connects us and gives us strength to share instead of hide.

Was there a specific moment, thought, or epiphany that helped guide you to a better place mentally and psychologically, or did it evolve?

It's been both, and of course it continues to evolve as we are all masterpieces in progress. But there was a specific time in my early twenties when I moved to Boston. Boston had been the place where my parents had taken me for medical check-ups because it was on the leading edge of genetics. It was really traumatic for me. I felt like a specimen. I felt like I was the description of my body. The doctors called it a birth defect. They pointed to things and said, "abnormal", "deformed." That became the definition of me. I didn't realize then that they were speaking about a condition. As a child, I thought the doctors were against me.

So when I moved to Boston it was this beautiful full circle. First it had been the place of incredible heartache; even the name

Boston used to get my adrenaline running. Then it became this place of awakening. I found a bookstore that was packed with self-help books and books on inspiration and motivation. I started reading themes like the power was within us, that our reaction to the outside world was the internal trigger that we could change. It was just negative programming.

This really resonated with me because I knew I was responding in a negative way. I thought it was because of my reality. But instead they were saying (the books) it's really your perspective. And when you are able to claim that, take responsibility for that, and say, 'I can undo this,' you'll see the progress and the change.

With fingers crossed and hope eternal, I did see changes. I read and read and read. I wasn't able to speak to my friends and share these things yet. It was very scary to show people who I really was. I had such rage built up, wanting to scream at the doctors, at the bullies, at my parents, all of it. It was just boiling; and it was released and relieved and comforted by these writers. I wasn't a writer then — that would be 20 years in the future.

I used to be afraid to just go out into the world in the morning because I didn't know if someone would be there laughing at me or asking me questions I couldn't answer. A lot of people have that, that anxiety, to step outside their door and not feel enough, or be afraid of failure. I would take Wayne Dyer's tapes in my Walkman, and instead of listening to my own criticism, I would listen to his tapes. His wisdom became part of my every step.

Those writers changed and opened my heart and my mind. I thought at that time it was an epiphany, a moment of ultimate change and transformation. Little did I know the path is long and there's a lot more that needs to happen than just an intellectual understanding, or a relief from the pain of childhood or our past wounds. There is this continual climb. It's not supposed to be a punishment as I thought it was. Now it's more of an excitement. When something seems negative my first instinct is to think something good can come of this because I've seen it now.

I've seen it in the biggest way where my dwarfism was the ultimate negative in my life and now it's become the ultimate teacher of how I really want to live.

What are your day-to-day coping skills that keep you afloat?

It's become an important habit for me to sit, close my eyes and breathe. Somewhere in that silence I start to see the craziness of my thoughts or that I need to feel something that I'm not feeling. Sometimes my busyness will eclipse what has built up over time and I just need to cry or write and express some rage that I know is mine; it's not really anybody's fault. It's that I've been plugging up the hole of expression. That moment of silence is really important.

While I drive I do deep breathing. There's something incredible about it. As I breathe in deeply and breathe out slowly, the relaxation in the body causes a relaxation of my mind and my heart. I can then see what I am still holding onto that isn't serving me well, or see how I'm looking at something that's causing pain or even causing me to move too quickly. What's the big hurry we're all in that's causing us to forget who we love, to not see the beauty on the side of the road?

When I take in that silence, I remember to tap into the shifts I need to make, the perspective that may be a little off. If we present ourselves differently in our world, then our response back is going to be more positive and more helpful.

I've learned not to take the world so personally. I see it as a place I'm trying to help, instead of that knee-jerk reaction toward a world that isn't taking care of me. That's a switch in my consciousness. For many years I was always looking for how I can be helped because I thought I needed help. Instead I realized I had something to give; it was me and my experience and my heart, and that was enough.

When we start to share who we are in that authentic place, others want to share too. So often it's communication that's the problem, not the issue; not my dwarfism, not lack of money. It's our response to it, and that can be changed, thank goodness.

What advice would you offer someone going through a difficult situation?

Ultimately our limitations really are self-imposed. It sounds like blame but it's not meant to be. It's meant to be empowerment; it's meant to be a catalyst to help us move forward. There is help everywhere, like the writers who I found, the authors who were like friends to me. What they said spoke to me so deeply. With technology there's no limit to the mentors we can find or the advice we can find. It's there when we're ready — it's waiting.

The incredible limitation leads to incredible freedom. There's always this light that comes out of darkness. I'm astounded that our life is about these extremes. But if we go from this place of heartache, we can be catapulted forward into the wholeness.

The silence I lived with as a child led me to understanding the power of communication. My differences that I felt isolated me, led me to a truer understanding of connection. The surface stuff — our bodies or finances or security — these things we are so distracted by are not who we are deep down. We have the seeds of opportunity within us that act like a slingshot forward so that we can transform that pain and be a billboard that shows it is possible. That's a really exciting place to be. To then be able to inspire someone who's been in your shoes and to know and really see them and say, "I know it hurts but it's going to get better."

It's really important to examine what we believe. I thought my beliefs were reality. I thought they were factual. I started to examine them and realized how many of them were negative toward myself and the world. I looked at the response in my life; my world was negative. I thought that was reality.

There was that crack in the armor where I said, "I've had enough of this and I may be a reason for why it got so negative." And that's hard to admit. It's an incredible strength to say, "So I was the one shoveling the dirt on myself. I'm going to start to dig myself out and see that I have this inner power that's going to keep blossoming, because now I see I do have responsibility and I do have the strength to lift myself out of this."

We can see that beliefs are a magnet for more of the same.

If we have a lot of negative beliefs, we're going to see a lot of drama and negativity around us. We can change it by changing our beliefs. We don't have to force the outside world to change; or in my case I couldn't change my body — there was no cure for that. I had to go inside and find out what else I could change; otherwise I felt hopeless. Discovering that power was huge for me.

I can be the one to transform my beliefs so that I can be a magnet for what I want, not what I fear or what I have already experienced.

Start to envision what you want to experience and then that will grow and bloom in your life.

Nothing Short Of Joy by Julie Genovese

è❧

Wayne Dyer said, "Don't believe everything you think." Our mind can be our harshest critic, turning and twisting everything toward the negative. We can change our mental channel though, by changing our perspective and focus.

It's a real shift to begin to view our relationship with life not from the perspective of what we feel entitled to, but rather asking what we can offer up to life. We make a decision to step up to the plate. No matter what we're going through there's always something we can offer. And giving of ourselves in some manner is giving to ourselves.

> *"The point is not what we expect from life, but rather what life expects from us." (Frankl 1959)*

So, how do we step up to life when it feels so overwhelmingly sad and painful? When we can't even face ourselves; when we want to hide away forever? We begin by confronting the monster of pain. It's huge and looming, and towers over us making us feel as miniscule as can be. And then it crushes us with its overbearing weight. But we have a basic instinct for survival. The choice then becomes, do we succumb to this monster, or do we fight, pull ourselves up and start putting ourselves back together from the inside out?

Strangely, perhaps, we need to start by giving expression to our pain.

Shutting out pain keeps it banging on the door. It wants to come in. When we face it and allow it entrance into us it eventually loses some of its potency.

In the poem, *The Guest House,* Rumi, the thirteenth century Persian poet wrote:

This being human is a guest house.
Every morning a new arrival.

A joy, a depression, a meanness,
some momentary awareness comes
as an unexpected visitor.

Welcome and entertain them all!
Even if they're a crowd of sorrows,
who violently sweep your house
empty of its furniture,
still, treat each guest honorably.
He may be clearing you out
for some new delight.

The dark thought, the shame, the malice,
meet them at the door laughing,
and invite them in.

Be grateful for whoever comes,
because each has been sent
as a guide from beyond.

Keeping the pain locked away within us keeps it festering and brewing. It then starts releasing its toxic gases in all the wrong places. It cries out to be heard, and we must share and give voice to our hurt. Surprisingly, when we make ourselves vulnerable by expressing our deepest fears, hurts, sorrow, we connect more to others and we feel less isolated. We end up feeling more supported just by shedding our bravado and being real. Can we dare do that?

*"Tragedy is a tool
for the living to gain
wisdom;
not a guide
by which to
live."*

Robert Kennedy

CHAPTER 20

Living Up to the Truth of a Tragedy

"You don't close the book on difficult things, not if you're a feeling person."

 Darin Strauss is an author and professor of creative writing. His most recent book is his memoir, *Half A Life,* a beautifully honest and examined look into an event that has forever shaped his life. In 1988 a high school girl was killed when she swerved on her bicycle into an oncoming car. That car was driven by another high school student, Darin Strauss. It was declared an accident and he was officially absolved of any wrongdoing.

And yet, how does one go on to live life carrying the weight of such a tragedy?

Please describe what you've had to overcome so that you could move on and live your life.

That's a long, complex, maybe impossible one to answer. And I fear that any response would be self-serving. But here goes. I felt guilt, which must have been less crushing than the grief the girl's family felt. And also less than someone who had been declared 'guilty' of something would have. (I was held to be blameless.) I felt confusion, too. (But so do most young people, though not to the degree I did, I'm sure.) So the answer would take a book to complete. (Go figure.)

What personal qualities have helped you carry on and move in a positive direction?

I'm not the one to say. But, I was proud to get a recent call from a fellow alum from my high school. She said that she'd gotten married in 2000, coincidentally the week when my first book, Chang & Eng, had come out. At her wedding, someone said: "Hey, did you hear about Darin Strauss?" That is to say, this someone meant to ask the bride: "Did you hear that Darin has a book that just got reviewed by Michiko Kakutani in the New York Times?" And the bride thought the question would be: Did you hear that Darin Strauss is homeless? Or a drug addict? Or something. She'd assumed that the accident would have destroyed me. So hearing that made me proud, though I'm not sure of what I should be proud. That I didn't become a total screw-up? Not sure if that is justifiable cause for deep gratification and self-worth.

Was there a specific moment, thought, or epiphany that helped guide you to a better place mentally and psychologically, or did it evolve over time?

I say in the book that "epiphany" is a false lead; that it almost never comes in the way fiction asks us to believe it does. And that "closure" is a smarmy term for self-help practitioners. You don't close the book on difficult things, not if you're a feeling person. What happens is we get better by slow degrees, by effort and luck. Not by lightning strikes.

What thoughts propel you forward?

That I did my best. That something was thrown before me, and I tried my hardest not to let anything bad happen. And that the bad happened anyway was, in fact, beyond my control.

In general, how have you managed to live beyond the tragedy and create a good life for yourself?

I let time do its slow healing work, and I found the moment when I was able to face it — and not the moment before — and then I did. I did face it.

What part does forgiveness play?

Not enough, for me. Forgiveness doesn't come easy. Maybe that's good. There can be a lot of cheesy self-regard in our drive to forgive ourselves, and not enough morality. We need to own up to the truth, or our self-forgiveness will be hollow.

What advice would you offer someone going through anything at all similar?

Seek help — good help. Write things down, and write them with honesty. But only when you are ready. Don't force yourself to.

But if you think you're able, then write — put things in order, one word at a time, and it will give you a power over the event, whatever the event may be. But don't lie to yourself; don't skip the parts that are unflattering. A piece of self-propaganda won't fool anyone, least of all you. And fooling yourself is not the objective. Finding the truth, and learning to have power over it — that's the goal.

Half A Life by Darin Strauss

ॐ

THERE IS NO FINITE POINT AT WHICH WE CAN SAY we have gotten over something. Sometimes, just when we think we have it under control, or think that we're better, something comes out from the sidelines and knocks us down. Hopefully, we can re-coup and regain our balance. We may wobble, but we don't go down. Such is the nature of pain and grief from situations that never go away, that cannot be fixed or reversed.

So, do we ever truly heal from tragedy? Gradually, the knife-like pain that disables our functioning starts to lose some of its sharpness and we begin to feel emotions besides the intense stabbing at our heart. A smile, a laugh, a warm feeling cautiously and lightly plays with us, teasing and teetering on the surface of our skin. The smile surfaces, the laugh surprises us as we hear it come out of our mouth, and the warm feeling feels foreign, almost like an alien. We don't quite welcome it but we let it in, and so begins our ability to feel traces of goodness, some lightness and — dare I say — even joy. And this process becomes the waves of life — sometimes crashing hard, but more often coming in smaller, gentler ripples. We go on, carrying both pain and joy together.

Facing the monster of truth head-on, taking responsibility, helps take away its power and minimizes some of its harsh effects. It's like pulling the curtains away from the Wizard of Oz to confront him, only to find out he's just a regular person like Dorothy and her buddies.

We can be our own worst enemies in terms of self-forgiveness. I know I am very hard on myself. After more than 30 years, I'm finally lowering my own hatchet — not quite buried it yet though — over having married a man whose writing on the wall spelled disaster while we were dating. I can't fathom how I allowed myself to remain and continue on into a marriage when all the bad and problematic signs had been played out during our engagement. What was my psychological make-up back then that kept my feet stuck to the pavement of marriage?

However, I got three of the best gifts of life out of the deal — my daughters. That doesn't help me personally though in dealing with my own shame over my decision back then. I find it hard to even recognize myself as someone who would have gone along with such glaring warning flags. As we know, decisions can have life-long ramifications, which play out in the present. Difficult situations continue to present themselves, reminding me of the poor choice I made.

Self-forgiveness and self-compassion are life-long endeavors for me, but one I continuously work at through readings, meditation, gratitude and mindfulness.

How good are *you* at self-forgiveness?

CHAPTER 21

The Messiness of Grief

"One Stitch at A Time"

 A nn Hood is the noted author of the best-selling novel, *The Knitting Circle* and the memoir, *Comfort — A Journey Through Grief,* along with many other books and short stories.

A few years ago I read her memoir, *Comfort,* about the tragic and untimely death of her five-year-old daughter, Grace, to a rapid strep infection. Despite the worst possible loss — that of a child — she has been able to rebuild her life and continue on in a productive and meaningful way.

What personal qualities have helped you carry on and move in a positive direction?

I think the curse of being an optimist has helped keep me moving in a positive direction. Also, I was raised to push forward, no matter what. I remember when I was nineteen and had mononucleosis, a virus sometimes known as the kissing disease. I came home from college to recuperate and my mother allowed me just enough time to do that. Then it was: Get off that couch and get back to the business of life.

Did you go through a period of self-pity? What helped lift you out so you could see beyond?

I think one big misconception about grief is that we move through it in some orderly way. Instead, it's a messy business.

191

Even now I can go through times of self-pity or despair, or any of the other emotions that together make up grief. Knitting, hugs, family and friends, my other fabulous kids, books — the same things that help me through every day lift me up at bad times. But I also learned it's OK to experience all the bad feelings too. Too often we beat ourselves up for feeling self-pity, or really any negative emotions. Part of moving through them is to feel them.

Was there a specific moment, thought, or epiphany that helped guide you to a better place mentally or psychologically?

Oh, no epiphanies, though that was what I hoped for — one THING that would make it better. Unfortunately, it gets better in baby steps, with lots of sliding backwards and dark periods. It's important in those times to know that it will be better.

What were/are your day-to-day coping skills that kept/keep you afloat?

I knit almost every day. In fact, I can tell when I'm going through a bad spell because I knit a lot. Luckily, I have a strong support system of friends and family and I call on them often. Knowing that I have a coffee date or a dinner set up with someone who understands helps me move forward.

What thoughts propel you forward?

I'm a take it day-by-day kind of person, so I tend to focus on what is up next rather than dwelling on large questions and projections. This attitude has actually helped me move forward. I wake up in the morning and take stock of that day. Usually that in itself propels me forward: get kids to school, dog to groomer, coffee date with friend, visit Mom, work on novel, speak at knitting store... that is my day today. And thinking about it, tackling it not only propels me forward but also makes me feel necessary, loved and creative.

In general, how have you managed to rebuild your life after your tragedy?

One stitch at a time. It is slow and often painful, and an ongoing process. Accepting that helps you do it. No magic wand or potion, no healing flash. Really it's just putting one foot in front of the other every day and going about the sometimes messy, sometimes glorious business of living.

What advice would you offer someone going through a very difficult time in their life, in the hope of being able to come out of the darkness intact?

Learn to tell people what you need. Do you want to be left alone? Do you want to visit a faraway friend? Do you want company? I have found that people want to help but don't know how. When I give voice to my needs, I am never let down.

Attack something new. For me it was knitting, which was anathema to anything I would have ever learned. For my husband, it was masonry. He re-did our entire front and back yard with gorgeous stonework, teaching himself as he went along. For others, volunteer work has helped.

Although I know how hard it is to remain hopeful during difficult times, find a mantra or talisman or something that you can hold or repeat when you feel hopeless — some tangible symbol of a better time.

Comfort — A Journey Through Grief by Ann Hood

ॐ

Dr. Tal Ben Shahar, a leading expert in the field of positive psychology states:

> *"All feelings flow along the same emotional pipeline, and when I block one set of emotions (the painful ones), I am also indirectly blocking others (the pleasurable ones)."* *(Ben-Shahar 2012)*

We need to let those awful feelings wash through us. It's OK; we don't die from them. As much as we don't want to confront those horrific feelings, we need to go through them so we can come through them. Feelings, like clouds, move and shift. Sometimes they're more opaque and weigh heavily on us; other times they're translucent and sit lighter. That is why the key is one day, one stitch at a time.

The hole in our hearts and souls can feel like it will remain forever. The future looks bleak and empty when we feel such loss — 'how can I go on?' But focusing on the immediate present, putting one foot in front of the other, is much more doable. We then start to add a link (a day) to our chain of life.... And we can see that we're doing it.

In fact, being very practical and getting back to the business of daily life can be soothing. Routines give us order and predictability. At least we feel like we have some control. When I'm in a bad way, I go for the house chores — folding laundry being my favorite. It's what I feel I can control when all else seems out of whack. And since it's mindless work, I accomplish something with no mental or emotional strain.

But this is not in lieu of feeling. We cannot busy ourselves forever so as not to feel. We can take healthy distractions away from it, but to avoid, numb and bury our emotion is a recipe for disaster since it will only come back to haunt us and wreak havoc — possibly in disguised ways.

What's your healthy distraction and outlet?

CHAPTER 22

The Education of a Tragedy

"Life happens — you're not immune to it."

G-Na Casazza, is a new and clearly talented filmmaker. When her grandmother was tragically killed by a drunk driver, G-Na turned to her passion of filmmaking and started working on a documentary to honor her grandma's life and educate the public on this deadly problem.

One Fatal Mistake premiered on the fourth anniversary of her grandma's death.

G-Na took her grief and channeled it into something for the living. What better way to handle death than to use it to improve life.

What has helped you carry on and move in a positive direction?

I was in film school at the time. I was taking a documentary class and at the end of the semester we had to come up with our documentary topic and an outline of how we wanted to make the film. Most documentaries work well when it's a topic that's very personal to you and that you really believe in. Considering this tragedy that happened, I thought why not re-live my grandma's memory and let it live on, and hopefully because of her tragic loss, something good can come out of it. I can make this documentary in order to help people.

I knew this would be successful because drink driving rates are so high. I knew I was able to take it to a whole different level. I was very driven to get this topic out there.

195

It's about my family but it's also a bigger picture. It brings you into one family to let you see the tragedy that struck so you can have some sympathy and hopefully think before you act.

I am very driven and when I want something and put my mind to it I end up doing it. I see this film being a lot bigger than it is now — and it got pretty big on Long Island — but now I want to take it national and let everyone see it.

What were your day-to-day coping skills?

It's very strange to see somebody one day and then never be able to see them again; talk to them one day and then never be able to talk to them again. One minute they're there and the next minute they're not. You don't really believe it at first; you don't really know what's going on — everything is a blur. My grandma died in November 2007. Then we had Thanksgiving and she's not there, and then we had Christmas and she's not there. It's things like that where it starts to become more real.

At first I wasn't dealing with me and my feelings — I was dealing with everybody and their feelings, making sure they're OK and getting through it with them, helping them. I was more of a comfort for everyone else. I'm the oldest grandchild out of ten.

My grandma passed away on a Sunday morning. To be honest, I went to school the next day.

Everyone deals with death differently. I noticed that all ten of us grandchildren dealt with it very differently. For me it was more of an acceptance — "OK she's gone, now what am I going to do, how am I going to turn this around?"

What propels you forward?

There's not a day that goes by that my grandma doesn't come into my mind. I had talked to her all the time. The day of the accident I talked to her for two hours on the phone. I was very close to her.

I've just always had that determination and will power to see my goal and go after it. That's exactly what I do every day. I wake up and have a to-do list of all the things I have to do for the day and I just go and try to accomplish it. I live day by day.

What advice can you offer others going through their own difficult situation?

From my perspective, let yourself grieve. Give yourself that necessary time to grieve.

Don't ever lose sight of your goal or whatever you want to do in life because tragedy hit. Don't let a tragedy stop you. Keep on going.

People die, tragedy happens. Your tragedy isn't going to affect anybody but you. People at first are sympathetic to you. Days, weeks and months go by and others forget, but you never forget. You never forget about that day or any of it. You have to keep that close to your heart and just keep on going.

You have to understand that you're going to fail, tragedy is going to strike again but you can't let that get you down. You never know when it's going to be the last time to talk to somebody.

I'm twenty-two years old; I still think I'm invincible. When I turned sixteen and I got my license, I never thought about death, about an accident. Even though you read about it, you don't think that's going to be you. You think you can't die. There's that sense that people need to snap out of and realize that life happens; you're not immune to it.

ža

GRIEF HAS MANY FACES. Throwing ourselves into a project that connects us with the loss can be very healing. (See Dan Habib's interview, page 149, The Vision of Inclusion.) We are creating a legacy and paying forward a life. We are also bearing witness in the hope of educating beyond a tragedy.

It's that purpose that drives our determination and focus — a purpose to create something good out of something bad so that suffering takes on meaning. When tragedy strikes, we need some kind of meaning in order to go on living. Viktor Frankl writes about the meaning of suffering as to "transform a personal tragedy into a triumph, to turn one's predicament into a human achievement." Suffering is certainly not necessary to finding meaning, but "meaning is possible even in spite of suffering."

We have to be careful not to bury our feelings in our work, but we can work through the grief as we create projects, organizations and causes out of the ashes of our loss. We must create meaning in our own way. It may not be something tangible. It may be more of an internal shift.

I wanted to do some tangible good with my miracle — my daughter's survival and complete recovery. I couldn't nail it. I tried a memoir — didn't make it. I thought about starting an organization but that didn't go anywhere. And so my meaning at the time emerged through taking on various personally meaningful projects, such as foster-raising a service dog, clowning — among other things — and my growth came through internal shifts towards living with more zest, appreciation, a sense of urgency and intention. I can honestly say I live a very 'rich' life as an outcome of Nava's miracle.

What, if anything, positive has emerged or have you created from your adversity?

Resources:

G-Na's documentary:
http://www.onefatalmistakemovie.com/

Mothers Against Drunk Driving: http://www.madd.org/

CHAPTER 23

Recovery Practice

"I decided to treat my physical and cognitive therapy sessions like football practice."

 While vacationing in Florida six weeks before college graduation, a repeat drunk driver lost control of his car and crashed into Steven Benvenisti while he was walking with his friends. His legs were crushed, his face smashed through the windshield and his body was thrown 70 feet. His prognosis was poor as he lay in a coma.

Upon a miraculous survival and complete recovery, he is fulfilling his promise to devote his life to ending drunk driving and helping those dealing with brain injury as a result.

He is most successfully carrying out his life's work and purpose. As an attorney, he represents DWI (driving while intoxicated), brain and personal injury victims. He's a motivational speaker and author of the book, *Spring Break: A True Story of Hope and Determination*. His Contract for Life between students and parents has effected positive change in the drinking and driving behaviors of teens.

What personal qualities have helped you carry on and move in a positive direction?

I would have to say my self-determination.

Upon awakening from my coma (after my accident) and realizing everything had been taken away from me because of a drunk driver, all I could think about was how great my life had previously been and how sad it was that my life would never be the same again. I was living with horrendous pain, my memory and cognitive abilities were significantly compromised and it was unknown if I would ever walk again. During those times I reflected on my past.

I remembered my high school football coach who tried to instill in us players the idea that if we wanted to improve any skill on the field, especially when we felt the urge to slow down and give up, we needed to use that as a catalyst to push ourselves twice as hard for as long as possible. And so every day when I ran and started to get tired and slow down, I used that feeling as a reason to push myself (twice as hard for as long as possible). As the football season progressed, my speed increased dramatically. I went from being one of the slowest runners to one of the fastest.

I realized while lying in my hospital bed that if I was able to improve on the football field simply by pushing myself when I felt like giving up, then why not apply that same determination to improving in my recovery. I decided to treat my physical and cognitive therapy sessions like football practice. Many of my therapists shared with me that they had never seen a patient more determined to improve than me. It was that determination that drove me to my full recovery.

Did you go through a period of self-pity? If so, what helped lift you out?

After awakening from the coma, I became more depressed than I had ever been. I was at the lowest emotional level I thought a human being could be at. Being happy again one day was so unbelievably far-fetched and unrealistic. I was told there would be little, if any, improvement. I had no idea how I could ever come close to being happy again.

The turning point in my emotional recovery was when I realized that my pre-accident happiness had nothing to do with my good health, my grade point average or even my social life. The only reason I was happy before the accident was because I chose to fill my mind with thoughts that put a smile on my face. In fact, the only reason anyone is happy or unhappy at any given time has little to do with their actual circumstances and has everything to do with what they're thinking about.

While hospitalized, as soon as I realized that being happy in the present moment simply involved changing what I decided to think about, everything changed. I realized most of my grief came from comparing myself to who I was before the accident and the fun life I was missing out on.

It wasn't easy, but instead of thinking of all the great times I was missing with my college friends, I thought about how nice it was to be with my family, to have a girlfriend I could talk to, to watch TV and eat whenever I wanted to. When I was in cognitive therapy, instead of thinking about how sad it was that I was no longer an active college student earning credits towards graduation, I thought about how cool it was that the more I read, the easier it was to understand what I was reading. Instead of thinking about how sad it was that I could no longer be the same athlete who won races, I made my new sense of athletic purpose trying to walk a little further on the parallel bars. Every time sad thoughts about the past, present or future would creep into my mind, I would force myself to think about things which put a smile on my face. As the months of my hospitalization continued, I gradually came out of my depression.

That way of thinking continued through my three years of law school and the decades which followed as an attorney today.

What were/are your day-to-day coping skills that keep you afloat?

After the first month of my almost six-month-hospitalization, I convinced myself that my life was being wasted away; that every day I was in the hospital was another day of my life being stolen from me. I desperately needed to change that way of thinking because if my condition remained permanent as the doctors said it would, then my entire future would be a complete waste as well.

I decided to transition my thinking into realizing that my hospital time didn't translate into time being taken from me, but rather as time being lived in a different atmosphere. I began to accept that the best place for me in my new condition was in the hospital and that I needed to view my hospitalization and therapy as my full-time occupation. With that change of thinking, I began to feel productive which dramatically improved my self-confidence throughout my hospitalization. It got to a point where it didn't matter if I 'got better' one day, as long as I felt that I was leading a productive life. Treating my hospitalization and therapy as my new 'job' made me feel more complete with a sense of true purpose.

What thoughts propel you forward?

Believe it or not, since my accident, although I plan for the future, I rarely think about it. After having almost lost my life at age 21, I realize that tomorrow is guaranteed to no one. The only thing that is real is right now. I live my life with the goal of being happy in the present moment, working hard and treating those with whom I come into contact with the utmost respect. I genuinely believe if someone wants to live a worthwhile and successful life, all they need to do is have a healthy and meaningful formula by which to live every single day, and opportunity and success will automatically follow.

What advice can you offer someone who's been in a traumatic accident, in the hope of rebuilding his/her life?

Regardless of whether they ever 'get better', it's important to find happiness given their current circumstances. When I learned the grim prognosis for those who sustained my kind of orthopedic and brain injury, I made up my mind that I couldn't base my happiness on hopefully getting better one day. That way of thinking meant there was a good chance I would never be happy again. What I described above and more at length in my book, is how I found the pathway to happiness. Simply put: your emotions are controlled by your thoughts.

Spring Break: A True Story of Hope and Determination by Steven Benvenisti

&⁏

WE ARE IN CONTROL OF OUR THOUGHTS. We can decide both 'how' to think of something and 'what' to think about it in the first place. If we notice that our thoughts are bringing us down to a low place, we can shift our focus — we can change how we view something. We don't have to buy into a victim mentality. That line comes up again, "Don't believe everything you think." Questioning our thoughts is described in the work of Byron Katie, known as 'The Work'. It's a method of self-inquiry which enables us to think about our thoughts and question their truth and validity. We know we all too often make assumptions that carry us along a path of misunderstanding and pain.

Grieving the loss of what we had or expected is the work we need to undertake in order to be able, eventually, to accept a new reality. 'Shattered dreams' — as Dr. Ken Moses a psychologist specializing in disabilities and loss, calls it — must be grieved through in order to free ourselves up and be able to connect to new ones. We must embrace our grief as natural; our working through it is our entrée back into the world, albeit with new parameters.

As we see from Mr. Benvenisti here, happiness is not based on circumstance. This is backed up by considerable research on our levels of well-being. For example, that pie by researcher Sonja Lyubomirsky which showed that only 10% of our wellbeing is determined by circumstance. And as Viktor Frankl came to discover from his horrific circumstances in the Auschwitz concentration camp in World War II, man is free to choose his response to his circumstance:

"Everything can be taken from a man but one thing: the last of human freedoms — the ability to choose one's attitude in a given set of circumstances." (Frankl 1959)

Understanding this means it's up to us to do our work from the inside out, to work on our minds, our emotions and our character strengths that can put us on the path to living well despite...

Resources:

Contract for Life:
http://activatingawarenessgroups.org/contract-for-life/

Byron Katie: http://thework.com/en ; http://www.byron katie.com/

CHAPTER 24

Breaking the Cycle of Parental Blame

"Life is a series of choices."

Mother daughter relationships are not always easy to navigate. They're the most basic human (and animal) bond, and can set the stage in a most profound way for our lives. Katie Hafner, journalist and author of many books, has written a memoir, *Mother Daughter Me*.

Does our past have to define our future? Must a troubled childhood create a troubled adulthood?

Give us a brief picture of your mother and your life.

The book (and my childhood) is about not being raised by my mom.

My mother was very restless. Let's understand, instead of blame. She was in a terrible position. She was very smart. There was the famous cocktail hour and she was — and this was not an advantage— very beautiful. She attracted men like it was going out of style. She was having affairs. She left my father and took us to Florida when we were little girls. She started this itinerant life, this anywhere-but-here kind of life; and pulled a lot of 'geographics' which is what alcoholics do when they think life will be better elsewhere. They make a physical move without making any internal changes, which is typical. This poor thing, she then decides she doesn't like Florida and takes us to California. The drinking gets worse, and by the time I'm ten it's so bad my sister and I get taken away from her. We get sent back to live with my father, his new wife and her three children. And that didn't go well. It was tough.

Having said all that, I still, all my life, held onto this fairytale-like view of how things could be between mother and daughter. I stayed in touch with her. I did not give up on her. When she went into a crisis in 2009, and my husband had died and my daughter and I were by ourselves, I told her to come live with us. I had this completely gauzy, magical view of how it could be; this nuclear family that I never had and that she didn't have. So she moved in but it completely unraveled very quickly.

Did you have unresolved emotions? If so, how did they reveal themselves?

I realized I had anger I didn't even know I had. I had to go into this in order to come out the other side. I thought I wasn't angry. Friends would say things about their mothers and I'd say to them, "You don't know anything about terrible childhoods, just get over it." I really was a lot more bitter and angry than I thought. She had been with us for maybe a few weeks and I started acting out in the worst way. I am not a cruel person but I started doing cruel things like ignoring her needs; nothing that would jeopardize her, but it was emotional. There was one awful incident. She had bad carpel tunnel syndrome. We were at a Trader Joe's and she was trying to reach a half gallon of Lactaid on a top shelf with her bad hand. Of course at any other time for anybody — and for her too — I would've immediately jumped and helped her, but I turned my back. What a cruel thing to do; I pretended I didn't see her reaching. I thought, "Oh, my gosh! What is my problem?" And that's when I started to write the book.

What qualities helped you carry on and move in a positive direction?

Roll of the genetic dice. My sister wrote me this poignant email questioning what it is that made us so different. It's like we were two rosebushes and we got the same amount of sunlight and the same amount of water yet we became completely different. She was probably born an alcoholic. She became one at a very young age. It's a really sad, sad story.

I developed this ability to distance myself from an early age, which made me a good reporter. I became a journalist at a young age and just observed, and still do. It gets me through a lot and always has. I would pull myself back.

I figured out a way to save my own skin. I knew how to look out for myself. There's a scene in the book where my mother sued for custody after we were taken away from her. A really smart, aggressive woman lawyer went after her in the cruelest way because of her lifestyle in San Diego and what she had taken us into. They had me draw a diagram of what it took for us to get to the bathroom, which meant going through my mother's bedroom. She often had men in that room. I drew it and explained that we would actually pee into a jar so that we didn't have to go through her room. They used that in court. It was incredibly painful for my mother to have to listen to and yet I knew that going back to that situation would have been really bad for me. That's what I mean about saving my own skin.

My late husband, who was an amazing person, loved me deeply from age twelve and we were together on and off all through this time. He knew how to love like it was nobody's business. He taught me some important lessons that my sister didn't get, in taking care of other people's hearts. I know it sounds Hallmark-card-ish, but it's very important to me now as an adult. I got a lucky break on that one, in Matthew, and his mother, who's a huge figure in my life to this day. He was like my savior and then he died.

Was there a specific moment or epiphany that helped guide you to a better place mentally and psychologically?

There was this moment when my mother tried to quasi-kidnap us and we made it back to Massachusetts with my father and stepmother. We got back there after the summer incident where she had decided she was going to get custody of us and hold onto us. I remember coming back to Amherst and seeing the freshly vacuumed carpeting and seeing the tracks across the carpeting and thinking, "This is order, this is stability." The cleanliness symbolized everything I needed in my life.

I've always looked for this picket fence thing. With Matthew I had it and really held onto it. I'm a big cook and I love puttering, and flowers. Everything that grounds a person. You know the image of freshly baked chocolate cookies — that's the epitome of it still for me.

What are some life lessons you've learned through the writing of your memoir?

It was writing the book that really helped me through a lot of this. I was like a lot of other women who blamed their mothers for pretty much everything. And that is so misguided. Yes, we are the product of the people who give birth to us and raise us. And there's this thing I didn't even know about before I started the book called multi-generational trauma, where whatever has happened to you, you pass on to the next generation and it's a very difficult cycle to break. I broke it with my own child, Zoe. Some might say I overcompensated in raising her, so sue me. I needed to come to terms with what my childhood had been and the kind of parent my mom had been. The book is a lot about forgiveness.

There's this one harrowing scene where I was married to my husband, Zoe's dad, and I have an affair. He confronts me and what do I do, I blame my mother. It's right then and there I think, "Oh my God, I can't blame my mother. I did this, she didn't tell me to do this."

I feel strongly about a few things that I learned through this whole thing:

Life is a series of choices. We go into these choices with our vision intact. Unless we're completely stupid or have this delusional thinking going, then we know what the consequences can be.

We can't spend our lives blaming our parents. You gotta take things on yourself.

What advice can you offer others to live well beyond their difficult past and not fall victim to it?

First you come to terms with it. Look it square in the eye and figure out what you're accountable for — what parts of it you're off the hook because it was beyond your control and what parts of it you have a say in — where you can make the choice to dwell in it and blame others for it, or not.

Mother Daughter Me by Katie Hafner

ॐ

BLAME EQUALS VICTIMHOOD; responsibility equals freedom. Living in blame, and certainly in past blame, keeps us stuck in victim mode. Taking personal responsibility for our own lives is a huge step towards freeing ourselves from this imprisonment. It is hard work though; excruciatingly hard to loosen and lift the heavy chain that keeps us in our place of comfortable victimization. And comfortable it is because maintaining the status quo is always easier, safer and requires far less work. Knowing that there may actually be things we can do to change our trajectory might feel scary as we enter into the unknown. But it is what we must do to grow ourselves into a better life.

Using the past as an anchor just keeps us stuck and miserable. It may explain our actions but it doesn't excuse them. Making the decision to do something different is the first step in lifting those chains and owning our lives. It's empowering to recognize that we can be the author of a whole new chapter.

We learn what we live, which is why abuse is often passed down to the next generation. This is considered to be multi-generational trauma, and is often called the cycle of abuse. To break this cycle we first need to become aware of its existence and then take steps to change our behavior. Working from the inside out to uproot the insidious patterns often requires the help of a therapist and the courage to look at our long-standing pain. We must be self-examining and not live on auto-pilot, pushing that same replay button over and over. Change the tape, change the person, change the life.

As Tony Robbins says, "Most people think the past equals the future. Of course it does — if you live there!" We don't have to live there. It is up to us and the decisions we make. The choices are ours. Remember — response-ability — our ability to respond is in our control.

CHAPTER 25

"A Mind Like Schwarzenegger's Body"

"Feel the fear and do it anyway."

Mark O'Brien and his girlfriend, Susan Fernbach, cuddle outside his iron lung at his apartment in Berkeley in 1997. (Mary F. Calvert/Staff Archives)

This interview is unusual in that the person of interest, Mark O'Brien, passed away. He was a writer, poet and social activist and is the subject of the movie, *The Sessions*. He lived in an iron lung due to having had polio at an early age. The focus of the movie was his determination to have sex be a part of his life. But his main purpose in life was advocating for inclusion. Humanity first, disability second.

This interview was conducted with Susan Fernbach, Mr. O'Brien's partner.

What personal qualities helped him carry on and move in a positive direction?

His sense of humor, his intelligence (I used to say he had a mind like Arnold Schwarzenegger's body), a kind of patient tenacity. He once said that what most people think of as courage is really an extreme form of patience.

How did he handle pity, from himself or others?

He turned it on its ear in his poetry and other writing, made fun of people's pity for him and his own self-pity. In *Breathing Lessons* and in *The Sessions* he, and the character based on him, somewhat facetiously blame God for his situation, making self-pity into a joke. However, his humor did not negate his feelings — it helped him cope.

What were his day-to-day coping skills that kept him going?

He learned to manage his attendants, hiring and firing as needed, giving instructions to them on how he wanted to be assisted. He learned a lot of these management skills from other disabled people in Berkeley. He learned gratitude, which helped him focus on the things that were going right, and he had a spiritual life connecting him to the Divine.

What thoughts propelled him forward?

He set projects for himself that he could accomplish — starting an essay, writing a poem or a journal entry — and the sense of accomplishment helped give him impetus to keep going. When he felt afraid or discouraged, he wrote down those feelings in journals or poetry to get them out of himself.

In general, how did he manage to build a productive and meaningful life?

He did things even though they scared him — "feel the fear and do it anyway" as the saying goes. He set goals and accomplished them. He built important connections within the disability community based on the "social model" of disability as a rights movement, rather than the "medical model" which defines a person only as a set of deficits or conditions. His disabled friends were very important to his self-image and in reducing his sense of isolation.

What advice would you give someone with disabilities so they can transcend their challenges and live their life to the fullest?

Take what society says about you with a grain of salt, especially the media's stereotypes. Don't allow them to pigeonhole you. Set your own goals and celebrate your accomplishments. Don't be denied a purpose for your life.

Read up on the disability rights movement and find out about the courage of people in wheelchairs who chained themselves inside San Francisco's federal building to demand enforcement of anti-discrimination laws. They are inspiring.

Join groups or online forums where you can communicate with other disabled people. You are far from alone. Mark used to say that everyone will be disabled if they live long enough.

Notes to those who love a disabled person:

Be honest and gentle with yourself about your grief. Their loss of ability is a loss for you too. Being a poet myself, I wrote down my grief about Mark's limitations into several poems.

You may feel like all that matters is your loved one's state of mind and rehab/goals/accomplishments. For a while, at the beginning of a disability, that may be true when everyone is in crisis mode. After a while, however, even though it's hard to do, it's important to reclaim some of your own focus, goals and projects. These can help recharge your batteries and help you feel good about something, especially amidst the grief that comes with loss of ability.

Although you may want your loved one to overcome his/her

condition, don't allow yourself to be made responsible for their state of mind.

Find other people with disabled loved ones. They understand the fatigue and grief that comes with the territory. There are many resources for this on the web for specific conditions and diagnoses.

If you find yourself in the role of caregiver, try to find support. Many senior centers or centers for independent living have resources like this.

How I Became a Human Being by Mark O'Brien

એ

DEFICITS, DISABILITY, ILLNESS — ALL SEEM TO DEFINE A PERSON. However, as we've seen throughout many of these interviews, there's a lot more to a person than what he isn't or what she can't do. We need to view a person through a much broader lens so we can see and embrace both the limits and strengths, and not allow the 'problem' to be the whole person.

My daughter Nava's voice came alive on the phone when she told me she had written her first check. This prompted her to ask if she could have her cell phone account put into her name so that she could pay her own bill. To derive such satisfaction, joy and pride in an achievement is to enhance her internal reservoir. This in turn adds to the richness, feelings of wellbeing and excitement of her life. We must pit each person's goals against themselves. For her, and me, this was a big deal; to revel in the accomplishment was a huge positivity enhancer.

We can strive to become our best. Oftentimes it takes tremendous mental strength to forge ahead way beyond our life challenges and limitations. Opening up our repertoire of options is key. Thinking out of the box can create new ways of being and living which allow the character strengths of resourcefulness, creativity, and problem-solving to be brought to the forefront and maximized. We all have them but we must call upon them. However, first and foremost, our responsibility is always to work through the loss and grieving emotions so as to free us up from the intense pain and enable us to see new possibilities.

People in such adverse situations, like Steven Hawking, a physicist with ALS disease who has lived way beyond what was medically foreseen, seem to go beyond humanity's normal limits in their capacity to continue living, growing and contributing to society. Once again we learn that a meaningful and productive life can continue on beyond adverse circumstances. Our response is the determining factor.

*"The best way out
is always through."*

Robert Frost

CHAPTER 26

Choosing Hope

"Choose to inhale, don't breathe simply to exist."

*"Go forth vowing to choose gently,
celebrating life each day.*

*Go forth vowing to choose wisely,
playing after every storm."*

From "Choice Vows" by Mattie J.T.
Stepanek in *Loving through Heartsongs*
(Hyperion, 2003)

How do we live on with huge holes in our heart, with deep pits of emptiness? Jeni Stepanek answers this in her incredibly courageous way as she lives on despite incomprehensible adversity. She lost her four children to a rare form of muscular dystrophy, from which she herself also suffers. Her ability to rise above these odds and create a life of meaning and joy is truly heroic and miraculous.

It's no wonder that her son, Mattie, became the inspirational peacemaker and poet who was chosen by Oprah as one of her "Most Memorable Guests". He continues to be a teacher to the world through his profound words of poetry, and Mom continues to carry on her son's philosophy of life through her own teachings and work directing the Mattie J.T. Stepanek Foundation, and spreading Mattie's message of hope and peace.

What personal qualities have helped you carry on and move in a positive direction?

Faith. I believe there is a higher power; that God is present amid suffering as well as celebration. People are quick to say "Thank you, God" when they win the game, but to say "Where was God?" when they lose the game — that's not what God is about. God is about being present with us in triumph and tragedy. So I have a very deep faith.

I also think I have resilience — which is not the same as optimism, as in 'just keep a stiff upper lip'. Resilience is making a choice to move forward despite the fact that in all probability I will be facing burdens that are balanced in with my blessings.

The third quality I have is an incredible community of support. If I can't find a reason to take that next breath with purpose, there are other people willing to offer me a reason. I just have to allow that.

A lot of people have a community of support and they don't realize it because they are not looking for it; they're not open to it. The easiest thing would be to just lie in my bed, miserable with my disability, miserable with my empty lap, miserable with what's happening if you look at the actual facts of my life.

But that's not what life is about. So it is a choice to seek hope in each moment; and sometimes I have to make that choice when I open my eyes in the morning, and then a gazillion times throughout the day. But that choice can only be made by me. And I've had times that there are people who would be there to help me, but if I'm feeling too miserable about myself or my life I don't always see the community of support that's out there willing to help. It really is a two-way street. It's not just about people giving; it's about being able to receive, and recognizing that we have something to give. Even as I sit here in a wheelchair and on a ventilator, I have something to offer. We have to do our work in it also.

Did you go through a period of self-pity?

No, I've never been through times of self-pity. I have been

through, and will probably go through, many times of misery though. And that's very different. I've never felt, "Oh, why me?" Pity is when you feel bad, you feel helpless, you do nothing and you don't seek answers. Misery is when your life has so many storms that it's hard to figure out how to "play after the storm", as Mattie's philosophy was, because the storm doesn't end. I've had my great share of miserable moments and I probably will have many more, but I go back to the blessings of faith and resilience, which is choosing hope, choosing to reflect God in the moment, and accepting a community of support.

What a great distinction between self-pity and misery; because self-pity keeps us in that hole and keeps us with the why's, but we can't answer the why's.

No, we can't. And it's OK to question why. Anybody who loses a loved one, or faces a personal tragedy, whether it's disability or loss of a job or loss of a friendship, anything that tears at your heart or your mind or spirit, you have a right to be sad and angry and to question why — or as Dr. Phil says, "You own your feelings." Sadness is real; anger, frustration, misery are real. But pity is just getting stuck in that and not looking to say OK, I didn't choose this life, but I can choose how I reflect this life on to other people and into the future in a way that still shows that God is present and life is worthwhile. In some moments it may not seem like life is worthwhile, but I know it is and this too shall pass.

Was there a specific moment or epiphany that helped to guide you to this better place mentally and psychologically, or did it evolve over time?

Largely it has evolved. I didn't suddenly go "Oh, my gosh! I just need to choose hope." It really is something that you grow in. We grow in faith, we grow in resilience and we grow in the community of support.

I do have to say I had many 'aha moments' with my son Mattie, right down to the final sentence he ever spoke within a couple of days of dying — "Choose to inhale, don't breathe simply to exist." He was quite worried about how I'd go on because I had said "You can't die, you're my everything. I love you, I adore you, you're my son, my student, my teacher, my playmate, my prayer partner, my best friend." We were very close. I had said, "You cannot leave me; I can't do this." But death got closer and closer. He was really trying to hang on for me. He looked at me and said, "Choose to inhale, don't breathe simply to exist." And I thought about it. It was about a day or so later and I looked at him and said, "You know what, I will choose to inhale. It won't be easy, but it will be worthwhile and I will be OK. You can rest." He said "Yes", and within minutes he was gone.

I gave him a gift that broke my heart but lifted his spirit.

What are your day-to-day coping skills that keep you afloat?

If I get stuck in a moment where I'm feeling pretty miserable I really try to stop, and instead of thinking about why I'm miserable and how miserable I am, I try to think about who out there needs something I might still have to offer. And it may be that I go through my email inbox and find somebody that I might not have given a long response, and I go back and take the time to answer at length. When I have time to be miserable, it means not a lot is happening in my life. I'll go back to things that are worthy in my life and give somebody something; I'll give them a gift, and that helps me realize I have something to offer.

That's one coping skill — to put my misery aside and deliberately choose to try to make some difference that is good for someone else.

Another thing I'll do is photography. I'll go outside with a camera and find things to take photographs of because I love amateur photography. And then I'll come back in and find Mattie quotes, and put them together and make gifts for people, such as stationery.

What thoughts propel you forward?

I wake each day with, "Thank You God, I woke up!" on my breath. When I wake up and realize, 'Oh my, I have a whole new day', I am thrilled. And I know I'm going to hurt physically, I know I'm going to miss my children, I know I'm going to wonder what happens if something unforeseen happens and I have an extra bill and I can't make ends meet this month. I still honestly wake up every morning going "Ah, thank you God, life is amazing. Thank you for giving me another day to reflect Your presence."

You can continue to feel like that despite losing so much?

Absolutely. That does not mean that I don't miss my children; that I don't cry. I would say I cry at least once every single day. I buried four children; I did not know I was passing on a disease to them when I was giving birth to them. I'm now dying from the same disease. I am divorced. I don't have a regular job. But then I think, 'Oh, my gosh — I'm awake, I'm taking a breath. I live in a beautiful house because of my son; I overlook a park named in honor of my son. I see what grew from his life. I'm not looking back on what was; I'm looking forward.' I am grateful for that.

A quote from Mattie that is in the book I wrote about his life (*Messenger: The Legacy of Mattie J.T. Stepanek and Heartsongs*) is, "If you have enough breath to complain about anything, you have more than enough reason to give thanks about something." When he said that age 10, after realizing that his body was dying, this is when I first started saying if I've got another breath, I'm going to use it to give thanks for something. There are mornings when I wake up and I say "Thank you, God", and I say "Please help me get through today and help me reflect that you're with us even when we're suffering." Because there are days with some extreme pain in it. Those are the thoughts that I wake up with to really start with appreciation.

It sounds like the biggest thing that keeps you going is such a strong sense of purpose and meaning.

Yes, but it's not like meaning and purpose are placed in front of my face and I just have to put my hands out and there it is. I have to search for it, I have to create it; I have to make meaning.

People will look at Mattie's life and say, "Wow, that's a life with purpose." I have a son named Stevie who died aged six months and two days. His life had just as much meaning and purpose. He had as much reason to be here as Mattie, who lived almost 14 years, as did my daughter Katie and my son Jamie. I have to search harder to figure out what is the meaning of life when a child lives for barely six months, and those six months are filled with suffering. But I guarantee you there was meaning and there continues to be meaning. Mattie was and is who he was and is because of his siblings. He appreciated life at a deep, deep level because he was the youngest. He had the gift of longevity because he was the baby. It's not that the first three came so that Mattie could live; but because the first three came, Mattie did live. We accept that, and celebrate meaning within that truth.

What advice would you offer someone going through a difficult time?

That's probably the hardest question of all. I'm good at telling you what I do, but to offer advice to others, I'd have to be in their mind and heart and spirit.

The best advice would be to know that you're not alone. Even if you don't know someone in your situation, there is somebody in this world that you may or may not ever meet that is feeling the same pain as you. You're not alone.

And secondly, there is something you can do with this moment that places meaning in some next moment; and maybe it's not meaning for you, maybe you're too much in pain to see anything good about your life. But there's something you can do for someone else. And that's what God calls all of us to do. Simply love your neighbors. And you can love your neighbor by doing something good even if you're feeling horrible. Maybe it's just simply a smile. Just know that you're not alone and that you do matter.

Advice is a very tricky thing. It makes it sound like I have the answers and I don't. And that someone can write out a prescription that heals all spirits. And there is no such thing. Advice sounds like it's a fix. If you offer advice and somebody is not ready for that, then they can feel even worse about themselves. I try not to offer advice. Advice is what you get from your doctor who can say, "Your foot hurts, here do this and it may help." Instead, I can offer a message; I can share what helps me, I can share what I've heard from others that has helped them.

Is there anything else you'd like to share or express?

There's something about Mattie's life, something about the way he lived and chose and spoke that inspires people to say, "I do have problems but I can make these same choices. I can think beyond myself; I can think into the next moment."

Messenger: The Legacy of Mattie J.T. Stepanek

ॐ

"It does not really matter what we expect from life, but rather what life expects from us. We needed to stop asking about the meaning of life, and instead to think of ourselves as those who were being questioned by life — daily and hourly." (Frankl 1959)

IF WE CAN LOOK AT OUR LIFE FROM THIS PERSPECTIVE, we may be better able to cope with what comes our way. To recognize that we all, no matter what our situation, have something to offer, is a very powerful thought — one that can help us persevere through our most difficult challenges. Thinking beyond ourselves, towards others, expands us and lifts us out of our own sad situation, even for a brief moment. It may then develop into something bigger than ourselves that gives us a reason to go on.

A purpose gives us the ability to transcend a challenge and keeps us going through the grind of daily stressors, frustrations and sadness. I made a conscious decision that I was going to raise Nava with the greatest potential of independence. That informed my day-to-day parenting. Going two to three times a week to her therapies for years was a big source of stress: coming home from work, running back out again, schlepping along my younger daughter, always rushing and piggy-backing appointments, trying to get it all in. But the overriding raison d'être was to build her up to be the best she could be, to function in her highest capacity and with the most independence. That was my parenting mission statement and that carried me through. That's not to say I snapped any less as I tend to be a yeller, especially when stressed and on overload. But, it meant I functioned with an awareness and intention of a larger goal that felt right and in alignment with my parenting values. That kept me going.

What does life expect from you? What do you have to offer? Uncover your goodness and strengths and let them shine.

Reference List

Stepanek, Mattie J.T. 2001. *Heartsongs*. New York: Hyperion

Resources:

Mattie Stepanek Foundation: http://www.mattieonline.com/ (Mattie's poetry books are listed there too.)

CHAPTER 27

The Practice of Life

"Everything is a daily practice."

After seeing the movie *Being Flynn*, I did what I always do — I looked up the real person. The movie is based on the memoir, *Another Bullshit Night in Suck City,* by Nick Flynn. The basic premise is that while working in a homeless shelter, Nick meets up with his estranged, homeless father. What follows is the poignant struggle of a son attempting to reconnect with a brilliant, grandiose and manic father, who also happens to be a perpetually aspiring writer.

Nick is a writer and poet.

What personal qualities have helped you carry on and move in a positive direction?

It's more of a support network that allows one to work through things. Friends and family; community. It's a group effort. It's recognizing the need for support systems. It's something that's actively done. You choose your friends and work on your family relationships and seek out those support systems.

Did you go through a period of self-pity; if so, what helped lift you out?

Everything is on a continuum. It's not like you're in it and then you're out of it. Some days you're in it and some days you're out

225

of it. When self-pity comes up you try not to water it and cultivate it. I don't think it's an emotional state that one should try to eliminate. It's a continuum. That's the model that's more useful to me. It's not good or bad. It's part of me.

Was there a specific moment or epiphany that helped to guide you to a better place mentally and psychologically or did it evolve?

I don't think there was much of an epiphany. I'm not much of an epiphany type of guy. I put one day in front of the other. Cultivate the things that are more beneficial to one's life than harmful. Again it's a continuum. It's not an 'either or'. An epiphany suggests an 'either or'; you're either healed or you're not healed. I think that's harmful.

What are your coping skills that keep you afloat?

I meditate. Certainly exercising and eating right. All that stuff. If you watch bad movies or engage in destructive behavior, you're not going to feel psychically sound. Everyone knows that and still does that anyway. You have to keep the balance right. I don't meditate and exercise and eat well all the time. You just do the best you can. Sometimes you're gonna' watch the dumb movie.

How have you managed to rebuild your life through your difficult childhood/young adulthood?

The main thing for me is I quit drinking and doing drugs. That was the main change. It wasn't an epiphany; it was more of a daily practice. That was a break from patterns like my father's. That was a conscious choice. I had few options; it was that or die. For me that's the main thing.

Everything is a daily practice. AA has that phrase, 'one day at a time'. It's basically the idea of being present in the moment. It's a Buddhist idea — that's what you have to do to write, to have a relationship — to see life as a daily practice. If there's any sort of little message here, this is something I think about.

What advice do you have for people going through a difficult situation?

Cultivate those support systems. And that's a daily practice too. Recognize that we're all connected in many ways. That's not so clear in the moments of suffering. But we need to try to hold on to that idea.

Another Bullshit Night in Suck City by Nick Flynn

༆

AT EVERY MOMENT WE HAVE A CHOICE. We even have the choice to choose to live like this, consciously aware that the choices are ours — how we react, how we act, how we hold ourselves, when we smile. We usually think of choices in terms of the 'biggies' in life — ie. choosing our friends, partners, jobs, where we live and so on — but in reality it's the most minute choices that can make all the difference in the quality of our life. When we live mindfully in the space of choice, we let go of being victims of habit and control — that automatic play button. We realize we don't have to simply hold that button down time and again. We can choose to make a new recording and be the creators of our life.

The victim mentality is one of no choice. Everything just happens. And the pity runneth over.

We start with the smallest of choices each day. Do we choose the morning stop at Dunkin Donuts for that sensory awakening and appealing delectable cinnamon bun, or do we prepare a two-minute microwave bowl of oatmeal with cinnamon and raisins, when upset about our weight? Being mindful of continuous choices gives us a much more proactive and purposeful way of living. For example, when going in for an interview we can walk in displaying our nervousness — shoulders slumped, hands fidgeting in our pockets, head down, hesitant gait — or we can intentionally decide to walk in with good posture, a smile and a steady stride. Amy Cuddy, social psychology researcher, says that when we put the action before the feeling it can actually trigger chemicals in our brain that then bring on the more positive emotions.

The choice is yours. You can choose to choose.

Reference List

Cuddy, Amy. 2015. *Presence: Bringing Your Boldest Self to Your Biggest Challenges.* New York: Little, Brown &Company.

Chapter 28

Drug Addiction

Many people take their problems and work to help others struggling with similar issues. The next two interviewees are advocates in their area of loss, pain and struggle: drug addiction. They are paying it forward and working to save lives from a life-stealing battle.

"When your past calls, don't answer. It has nothing new to say."

Unknown

The Creative Recovery Process

"Surrender was the beginning of the win."

Many of you probably know these oldies but 'greaties' songs: "We've Only Just Begun", "Rainy Days and Mondays", "Evergreen", and "Just an Old Fashioned Love Song".

Paul Williams is the talented singer, songwriter, composer and actor who wrote these hits, among many others.

He says:

> *"You know you're an alcoholic when you misplace a decade and I did."*

Mr. Williams overcame his addiction to alcohol and drugs and is now a passionate advocate in the recovery movement. He's a testament to the strength, power and ability of the human being to face the demon head on, work through it and grow beyond it towards a renewed life of meaning and joy.

What personal qualities helped you carry on and move forward in a positive direction?

I went to nine schools by the time I was in the 9th grade. A construction brat, we moved often. I was always the new kid in school and the littlest. My sense of humor became a defensive tool that served me then, and I think served me well during my adult years. And what would probably be described as 'magical

231

thinking' may have been a big plus. I didn't know I couldn't do so many of the things I've been successful at doing. That's an odd sentence I know... but that kind of belief that I had something special to give, worked in supporting my belief system from the very beginning. My career as an actor failed so I started writing songs. Didn't know I couldn't so I did. Had never scored a film but didn't know I couldn't so I did. I've been very fortunate.

Did you go through a period of self-pity? If so, what helped lift you out?

Never. I've always felt that the next great opportunity was right around the corner. There was of course, in the middle of my addiction, a period when I wasn't thinking about anything but getting the next drink or hit of cocaine. My 'psychic and spiritual arsenal' was closed for repairs for about a decade.

At this point in my life I live in gratitude and trust. This book that Tracey Jackson and I wrote, has been a chance for us to share the mind-set and the tools that have worked for me for the last 23 years of sobriety. They are simple applications of a way of living that have restored me to a place where I am content in this perfect 'now' and yet expecting the best of the future.

Was there a specific moment, thought, or epiphany that helped guide you to a better place mentally and psychologically, or did it evolve?

Surrender was the beginning of the win. When I quit fighting the drugs and alcohol, admitted I was powerless over my mind-altering substances, I began to grow emotionally and spiritually. I discovered the writings of Emmet Fox and Ernest Holmes, did some serious therapy and became active in the recovering community. Found safety and comfort in the center of the herd.

What were/are your day-to-day coping skills that keep you afloat?

I keep going back to gratitude. It's become a natural state for me. Prayer has a playfulness for me. Mental health has real elasticity. If I have a moment that feels out of balance, angry or defensive, it leaves me quickly. I stay active in the recovering community, speak often and try to quiet myself enough to listen to the music of the day. And I'm not speaking of the radio.

What thoughts propel you forward?

Again, it's the lack of thought sometimes that allows me to move forward. I run every morning for about two miles. It's always different. Sometimes I slip into a blank space that's meditation at its best. And sometimes I can't wait to get back to the computer to get my thoughts down. The creative process is a constant stream that I think we can all dip our buckets into. If you refuse to believe the "you-can't-do" gremlin in your head, or that family member or friend, if you stay positive, realistic but open to the possibilities, I believe we all can have powerful creative lives.

In general, how have you managed to rebuild your life through and after your addiction?

I started out by walking away from music and the biz. I concentrated wholly on my recovery. People would ask if I was writing and I would tell them "No, I'll write when the passion returns." And it did. In the meantime I went to UCLA for a year of study at their Alcohol and Drug Counseling program, went to work for the Musician's Assistance Program as a counselor and built a solid foundation for my sober life. A few hours every morning volunteering at hospitals and running groups carried me through the early years. Then Paulie Lama emerged. I'm sure of one life I saved — my own.

Trusting in the future is easier now with my personal history. I couldn't have planned for the life I have today. Looking back I understand that there's really no reward for worry. Stay loving, celebrate peace and trust. The Big Amigo has always provided in the past and will in the future.

What advice can you offer someone going through this kind of struggle, in the hope of coming through it intact, with the ability to live a flourishing life?

Forgive the language but, you can't save your ass and your face at the same time. Get honest. When I hit my knees, prayed for guidance and — this is the key — when I turned to another group of human beings and said, "I'm dying. I don't have a clue about how to save myself. Will you help me?" When I got honest and egoless, I found the help I needed. If you're in trouble with any addiction — drugs, booze, sex, food, gambling — don't try to handle it alone. Seek the help that's out there and begin to rebuild the life you deserve.

Gratitude and Trust: Six Affirmations That Will Change Your Life by Paul Williams and Tracey Jackson

ò&

ASKING FOR HELP IS NO EASY TASK. But before getting to the asking, we have to acknowledge and admit to ourselves that we even need the help. It means we have to push through that window of denial and oftentimes hit our lowest point where we finally say "I can't do this anymore."

Serving others from the depths of our pain and struggle is a win-win. Those coming through their pain pay it forward and bring their personal struggles, stories and compassion to others going through similar circumstances. We all need to know we matter and are significant in some way. When we are drowning in pain and hopelessness, and feeling useless and bereft of purpose, knowing we can make a difference in others' lives can be a life preserver which brings us back to the shore of our life.

Prescription Drug Overdose

"Learn a new way of communicating, and love them, because I promise you right now they don't love themselves."

Shannon Rouse Ruiz has become a fierce advocate for putting an end to medication abuse. She is truly inspirational in that, despite going through every parent's worst nightmare, she has been able to continue on beyond her tragic loss towards renewed meaning and purpose.

With the heartbreaking death of her teenage daughter, Shannon went on to start P.E.A.C.E. — Prescription Education Abuse Counseling Empowerment.

This is a growing problem that needs continued education, awareness and attention.

Would you share some background on your daughter's life/death, to allow us to know her a bit?

Kaitlyn was a hard-working 16-year-old. She had been active in soccer and competitive cheerleading. She held a job and maintained an "A" average. She had a great personality, and to know her was to love her. She had a big heart for people. During cheerleading practice when Kaitlyn was in 8th grade, she tore her ACL (Anterior Cruciate Ligament). After surgery, she was prescribed pain medicine.

After Kaitlyn recovered, she tried to go back to cheering, but couldn't get her knee to work the same as it used to. She was left without any sports or activities. She felt left out during her recovery and lost connection with her friends. It is very hard when you are in middle school and your whole world gets turned upside down, especially when you have to find new friends.

Kaitlyn struggled with prescription addiction for two years. The first year we had no idea. The signs were there, but the last thing a parent wants to do is admit their own child is dealing with drug abuse. In 2010, things had gotten out of control. I was being called to pick her up from the police department, which became a normal thing for us. Because she was a minor and looked cute, they kept sending her home. I can't tell you how many times I begged for help! I ended up charging my daughter with assault. As bad as I felt, I took a deep breath and thought that everything was going to be OK. Finally!

Kaitlyn was ordered to go to rehab for 120 days and sat in juvenile hall for 29 days before a bed became available. As bad as I hated for her to go, I actually felt a sense of relief.

On March 9, 2011, I went to Greenville to pick her up. We all knew she wasn't ready to come home but our hands were tied.

On June 23, 2011 Kaitlyn was pronounced brain-dead. Because of a combination of Fentanyl and Xanex, she overdosed and went into a chemically-induced coma. She stopped breathing and choked on her own vomit. This cut off blood flow to her brain and caused it to swell. This led to her brain death.

We were told that because CPR was started early, we could donate her organs. Only 2% of people who die are able to donate and she was a perfect candidate.

Looking back to June 20, everything seemed to be perfect. Only God knows why Kaitlyn chose this day to relapse. This one bad choice has not only affected her, but everyone in her life. She left behind a mother, two sisters, a grandpa, two nephews, a boyfriend and many people who loved her.

What personal qualities have helped you carry on and move in a positive direction?

I would have to say my faith. After my mother was diagnosed with terminal cancer, I was her caregiver. It truly tested my faith. Her courage and will to seek God without complaint strengthened my belief that everything happens for a reason, and we are a part of a bigger plan.

Was there a specific moment, thought, epiphany that helped guide you to a better place mentally and psychologically, or did it evolve?

The night of my daughter's accident, it was like God had his hands on me. When God speaks to you, you just know that you know. One week after her death I was thinking about events that had happened and it was like Kaitlyn put closure on certain things, and I asked God what I was to do with this. All I knew was to take this tragedy and educate kids and their parents.

What are your day-to-day coping skills that keep you afloat?

I cry daily. I tell people I work with to just let it be and I use it to fuel me to make a difference.

What thought propels you forward?

I did not want another child to suffer with addiction or another parent to have to bury their child!

In general, how have you managed to rebuild your life after your tragic loss?

I focus on community change. I have dedicated my life to help stop medicine abuse. I have also changed the way I communicate with people, especially my children. I don't tend to take things as personal attacks. I started the P.E.A.C.E. Foundation. It's a non-profit organization. Our mission is to educate the public about the dangers of prescription drugs and empower them with the knowledge to recognize and stop abuse before it starts.

I am the coordinator for my county's substance abuse coalition. I sit on various councils, all in the hope of making a difference.

What advice can you offer someone going through a tragic loss in the hope of coming out of the darkness intact and towards the light once again?

Look up! Let God be your comfort. If you have a loved one suffering from addiction, realize it's not about you. Their brain is chemically altered and they are not the same. Don't give up! Learn a new way of communicating, and love them, because I promise you right now they don't love themselves. They want to be that little angel again and they just don't know how or where to start.

ક

HAVING A PASSIONATE CAUSE CAN KEEP US GOING after horrific loss. Living on and transcending tragedy by serving others creates meaning out of suffering. This can make all the difference in the world between carrying on and crumbling under the heavy weight of loss and sorrow.

Of course, not everyone creates a cause to work for. But connecting to some purpose is a huge factor in living on beyond loss and adversity. We need to have something to wake up for every day. When our lives are changed drastically by awful circumstances, we are called upon to meet the pain and sorrow of that change by recreating our lives and finding new reasons and new ways to continue on.

As Nietzsche said, "He who has a why to live can bear almost any how."

Resource:

Website — Partnership for Drug-Free Kids: http://medicine abuseproject.org/

CHAPTER 29

A Cause Beyond Oneself

"The best and only way to get over depression is to get over yourself and do for somebody else."

Robin Smalley is a woman who has turned her personal losses of both family and friends into a huge gain for world health — the elimination of pediatric AIDS. She has rebuilt her life, or should I say created a completely new one, by serendipitously discovering her passion of serving other mothers. Ms. Smalley co-founded *Mothers2Mothers,* a South African NGO (non-governmental organization) providing education and empowerment for pregnant women and new mothers with HIV/AIDS. She is the international director of this nonprofit that is tirelessly working to prevent mother-to-child transmission of this virus in Africa.

What personal qualities have helped you carry on and move on in a positive direction?

I think I'm a big one for denial. Without being funny truly, I'm sort of like a teenager who never really believes anything bad is going to happen to them. With my breast cancer, where everybody else was so worried and looking at me like I was about to die, I never felt like this was going to be a life-changer or life-ender. I've always been the person to do what has to be done and get on with things. I've never been one to dwell. For me it was more inconvenient than anything else — like "What do you mean I have to have radiation every day for nine weeks? I don't have time."

At the beginning when my stepfather went, I could rationalize that he was ill and it was for the best.

When my mother died, it was horrible. She was very young and it was unexpected. I remember at the time thinking, "I'm never going to be able to hum again." For months it was like my throat closed up. The music would play and I couldn't physically hum to it. I felt like my chest was never released. But it's true what they say: everyday is better than the previous one.

I've always been a really positive thinker and been one to count my blessings. I felt incredibly blessed. I had parents who loved me. I had difficulties in my childhood but I always had a roof over my head and food to eat, and I got a good education. I felt really lucky. I came from a fairly poor background. Summer fun was playing with the fire hydrant in the Bronx. I'd look around and say "Wow, I have so much to be grateful for."

When my mom went, I kept relying on that; I kept saying, "OK but I had her. I had her for my forty-seven years. Look how lucky I am." It was really hard but you get through it.

Then when Karen, my best friend died, all of that deserted me — all that positive outlook, the counting of blessings — it just knocked me down. It was the first time in my life I wasn't able to find the bright side. Even when I was going for all my breast surgeries, I'd say, "But the surgeon's cute." There's always something. But when Karen went, it just broad-sided me. You don't expect to lose your best friend, your peer, and she had two children. It threw me into that whole thing, "It's not fair, it's not fair." When our kids say things aren't fair, we tell them, "Well life's not fair, get over it." So I was saying, life's not fair and I couldn't get over it. I didn't recognize myself. That was the scariest thing. I didn't know who I was if I couldn't find a bright side.

Was there a specific moment, thought, or epiphany that helped to guide you to a better place mentally and psychologically or did it evolve?

When Mitch, Karen's brother, invited me to come to Cape Town, South Africa, I thought that was the craziest thing. I couldn't even get out of bed. My husband was really concerned. I have a family history of clinical depression; never me personally, but my mother, my brother, they had depression. So my husband made me go.

My first day there I was meeting women who were so extraordinary and so brave and had so much spirit and joy where they had no reason to be joyful. These were women who lived in a cardboard shack with no electricity, no water. They were alone, they had AIDS; they were as down as I could imagine. And yet they were finding the bright side. They were finding things to get up in the morning for and they would sing. And I remember thinking, "My God, it took me over a year before I could sing after my mother died." They got to the clinic and they'd dance as they prayed. It was like a bucket of cold water. It was my first day there. I knew nothing about Africa, nothing about AIDS. I called my husband and I said, "I have to do this, we have to move here." My husband shockingly said OK.

Literally a month later we packed up the kids, the dogs and the house and moved. It was the absolute best thing. Karen and my mother had been very close. I believe the two of them made this happen. I've always thought they knew this was the right thing for me. It all just came so easily. There were all these things — if this doesn't happen we can't move, and on and on. But it all just fell into place.

In retrospect, it continued to do so. People thought I was insane. I quit my job, my husband left his work — we had nothing to go to. We were doing the program out of Mitch's car. We didn't have anything but a great idea. Within seven years we built it into a 20-million-dollar-business that's the largest employer of HIV-positive women in the world. It was something that needed to be done. What a gift I was given — to find the passion of my life at 48-years-old when I'd had a successful career. I won the awards; I was making good money as a television director. But it was a job; and it was fun. But I've found something that is truly a blessing. It's been a life-changer for me and my family.

All of a sudden I was in this place. I didn't have time for grief. I was learning so hard, so fast, it felt like my head was going to explode at the end of the day. I felt like a newborn must feel but can't articulate it. I was learning so much and it was so exciting. It got me using my brain. You get to a certain point in your career that you simply know how to do what you do. What people don't always know is that the skills they have can be used in so many ways. If you had asked me in a rational moment, "Do you have skills as a TV director that are applicable to running a non-profit in Africa for AIDS?" I would've said, "Are you kidding me!" Can you imagine two things more different? I would venture to say that any skill anybody has, has way more applications than they're giving themselves credit for.

I felt my mother and Karen there so strongly supporting me. I missed them but I wasn't grieving.

When you're focused on that much positive, there's just not a lot of room for the negative. There's only so much you can do at one time, and I don't think you can do both of those at the same time. I'm such a believer now; I know it's a platitude, but the best and only way to get over depression is to get over yourself and do for somebody else. We do for other people because it makes us feel good. Anybody who says otherwise is fooling themselves. And you can't feel bad and good at the same time.

Ask any young person, "What do you want to do when you grow up?" You want to make a difference. If you feel you're doing that, then nothing makes you as happy. If you're feeling that, then you want to get out of bed in the morning.

Did you go through a period of self-pity?

I don't think so. I went through tremendous sadness and loss and loneliness. Even at the worst of it I knew that you can always look around if you keep your eyes open and say, "There but for the grace of God go I". I have a beautiful family and two healthy children; no, I could never do the self-pity thing.

What advice would you give someone going through loss?

Look to help somebody who needs some help. I really feel the best way to deal with grief is to give to somebody else, anything.

My father passed away in January. I found this piece, (I don't even know where it's from) that I'm going to read at his unveiling. It says:

> *"Now that I'm gone remember me with smiles and laughter. And if you need to cry, cry with your brother or sister who walks in grief beside you. When you need me, put your arms around anyone and give to them what you need to give to me. There are so many who need so much. I want to leave you something, something much better than words or sounds. Look for me in the people I've known or helped in some special way. Let me live in your heart as well as in your mind. You can love me most by letting your love reach out to our loved ones; by embracing them and living in their love. Love does not die, people do. So when all that's left of me is love, give me away as best you can."*

That's it. And that is my advice. Stop thinking about yourself and think about somebody else and it is the best healer.

Please give us an overview of this global life-changing organization, Mothers2Mothers.

Mothers2Mothers (M2M) is an African-based not-for-profit organization which recognizes that women need to be at the heart of efforts to end pediatric AIDS and create healthy families and communities. We believe that employment is empowering, that education is essential for better health, and that by investing in women, we are investing in the future.

A simple solution to a complex problem, M2M trains and employs local women living with HIV to work alongside doctors and nurses in critically understaffed health systems as 'professionalised' members of the healthcare team. These "Mentor Mothers" provide women with essential health education and peer support to access healthcare early, follow their treatment, and stay in care so they can protect their babies from HIV infection and keep themselves and their families healthy.

Mentor Mothers also work in communities as frontline health workers, reaching out to women who have not yet come to health facilities, to encourage them to access care for themselves and their families, and following up with women who have stopped treatment in order to get them back in care. Mentor Mothers fight stigma through example and are role models in their villages, townships and communities.

They also offer education, support and referrals on other critical health challenges including TB, malaria, family planning, cervical cancer, nutrition, and gender-based violence. Maintaining contact with clients over the long term helps ensure they are taking their medications, testing their babies for HIV at six weeks and 18 months, and starting them on lifesaving treatment in the event they are positive.

Since our founding in 2001 at one Cape Town health centre, Mentor Mothers have reached more than 1.3 million HIV-positive mothers across Africa. We are committed to reaching 1 million more, and bringing health and hope to more women and their families.

እ

SOMETIMES OUR CALLING CAN COME OUT OF THE DEEPEST, darkest place. We need to be open and receptive to recognizing it, otherwise it can just as quickly pass us by. Being stuck in our own mire keeps us closed off to all other possibilities. Working through the pain and difficult emotions ensures that we do not remain sealed off. As the great American poet, Robert Frost said in his poem, A Servant to Servants, "The best way out is always through."

Resource:
Organization — Mothers2Mothers: http://www.m2m.org/

CHAPTER 30

Limited Movement Yields Unlimited Possibilities

Limited in movement but unlimited in spirit and potential, these next two interviewees have grown way beyond the confines of their wheelchairs towards great heights and depths of heart. They both live lives of significance, impact and service to others.

*"Self-pity
will keep you
immobilized so
that your future is
no different
than your past."*

Unknown

No Room for Self-Pity

"It takes strength to look someone in the eye
and say please help me."

Dr. Daniel Gottlieb is a psychologist, author and radio talk-show host in Philadelphia, PA. Thirty-six years ago he survived a horrific traffic accident; he woke up as a quadriplegic.

What personal qualities have helped you carry on and move on in a positive direction?

First and foremost was a loving, supportive family. Second, I had a large support network; I was always a social animal. Third, I had a career to go back to where I could help people, and the skills I needed to return to my career were unimpaired. In addition to that I had wonderful insurance and that's a big factor. I was able to have nursing care at home and still do; I was able to get top-of-the-line wheelchairs, vans, and convert my house. That's a big deal. So I had all those things going for me.

I think my learning disability helped because I always saw the world a little bit differently than a lot of other people. When I began to fail in school in the third grade I was told I was either lazy or not very bright. I felt so much shame that I felt different than everyone else. Everyone looked the same but I knew I was different. It was so lonely and scary for that little boy. Soon I discovered that my peers really liked me and from the time I was ten years old, confided in me about their lives. Obviously a budding young psychologist, but I don't believe this would have happened if I'd felt like I was like the other kids.

I was always a compassionate person. Because of my personality, right after the accident I was able to sit with people and listen to them, and people were more open with me than ever before. They felt safer with me than ever before. And because of the kind of person I was, I was very open about my vulnerability. I talked about my pain, my suffering, my fear, my internal life.

So I think all these things helped. It was my ability to connect with people.

Was there a specific moment thought or epiphany that helped guide you to a better place mentally and psychologically?

The first thing I had to decide was whether or not I was going to commit suicide. And I told my family I was going to wait two years and then decide. That epiphany was one of the most important in my life. But I knew when I said, "I want this, I want that, give me hope that I'll walk or that I won't be so sick" the voice back said, "No. No, hope. Live or die; choose this life or not." And I chose life, and I didn't choose it because I was strong. I chose it because I'm a being and that's what we do. For 98% of us, given the choice, we choose life, regardless. So I'm no hero.

What I have learned is that the more I've loved, the more I love. Any emotion, any behavior can turn into a habit. Hatred and despair are habitual reactions. And so is love and gratitude. And the more you love, the easier it is to love.

I am not at all confident that I'll be alive to see the spring. Given that, this day is pretty precious. I don't want to make myself out be the Buddha, because I ruminate with the best of them.

Did you go through a period of self- pity? If so, what helped lift you out?

I don't do self-pity; I do sadness. I've had three or four episodes of major depression, but that's way different from self-pity. I don't do the 'why me'. Although I do — I do the 'why me' but I do it on the other side of it. I look at all I have in life; why me, what have I ever done? I look in my refrigerator, it's full. I've got a comfortable home. It's freezing outside and I'm sitting here warm looking out a beautiful window. What have I done to deserve all these blessings?

What advice can you offer people going through difficult situations?

When I'm in a dark hole, I want someone who loves me enough to sit there next to me and not tell me there's light on the other side. Words are not going to do anything and 90% of the time they're going to be patronizing. They're also going to be a by-product of your own anxiety and helplessness. Just sit with me. Just have the courage to try to fathom what I'm experiencing.

One of the things I've learned is it takes strength to look someone in the eye and say, "Please help me." Most people think it's the opposite.

Pain heals on its own. We can do things to make it worse. You can pick at a scab or you can keep it in the dark, pretend it's not there. And you know what wounds do when they're in the dark. They just fester and get infected.

The Wisdom We're Born With: Restoring Our Faith in Ourselves by Daniel Gottlieb

ॐ

How do we sit with those in pain? How do we support them? By just 'being' and not looking to fill the silence or pain with words that may betray the reality of the sufferer. By holding their pain and letting their presence keep you connected.

Vulnerability is the way to hold on to grace. It connects us intimately with others. It helps us heal emotionally, to strip away the layers and get to the real raw deal of our truest self. It's our close and 'real' connections that keep us from feeling alone and alienated. But letting down our guard is scary, and for many, holding on to a mask of bravado appears to be a protector. However, in reality it's a barrier. It keeps us emotionally distant.

It takes strength to be vulnerable, to confront the deep abyss of sadness and fear, to express those deepest and most basic human emotions: heart-wrenching anguish, terrorizing fear and the bottomless hole of sadness.

Can you reveal your true self in your pain and sorrow?

Can you be with others as they reveal theirs?

Roll Across America

"It never crossed my mind that being in a wheelchair is bigger than me as a person."

 A while back my town made the news for something uniquely wonderful. Yes, a good piece of news for a change. A man, whose life was forever altered by a tragic car accident which left him a paraplegic, came back home on a triumphant mission. Gabriel Cordell (real name Suheil Aghabi) rode cross-country in a standard wheelchair. Starting out in California, it took 99 days and 3,100 miles to roll into his hometown of West Hempstead, New York.

His experience shows us there is no limit in life. We are capable of far more than we think, despite what we may consider insurmountable obstacles. An actor by trade, he's an inspiration by character.

What personal qualities have helped you carry on and move in a positive direction?

Ever since I was young I was instilled with a strong work ethic. I started working when I was thirteen years old. That showed me what it takes to be successful and how much hard work it is if you want to achieve something. I think I'm stubborn. In some ways it's good to be stubborn and in some ways it's not. In relationships it's not, but for personal goals it's absolutely a positive to be stubborn because you will be relentless until you achieve what you're after. Also tunnel vision: when I put my mind to something that means so much to me and that is difficult, to achieve it I put all my focus on it. I put on my blinders and I just move ahead and I don't take no for an answer.

Did you go through a period of self- pity? If so, what helped lift you out?

I've never had self-pity because of my accident. I've had self-pity when I decided to check out of reality and go into a lifestyle that had nothing to do with me being in a wheelchair, but rather with me being unhappy with where I was going. My rehabilitation was in the Rusk Institute at NYU. I was fortunate enough and stubborn when I just turned twenty-two, and I was put in the adult unit in a room with two men on life support. This was where I was supposed to rehabilitate, not just physically, but mentally and emotionally. I said, "I will not allow you to put me in this environment." I got transferred to pediatrics, and from day one there I realized how fortunate I was to have had twenty-two years of what they call 'normal life', and there was no pity. How could I pity myself when those babies and children would never have the chance to know what normal is, and I'd had twenty-two years? That played a big part in why I didn't feel bad for myself. Those children gave me so much strength and showed me not to pity myself.

Was there a specific moment thought or epiphany that helped guide you to a better place mentally and psychologically?

There wasn't really one moment. I never allowed myself to think I'm less of a person for being in a wheelchair. I never let my physical status dictate the way I lived my life. It never crossed my mind that being in a wheelchair is bigger than me as a person. When I was lying on the ground, after I opened my eyes, I just knew I was paralyzed. I remember the thought that came to me as I lay there was, "This is the vehicle that's going to allow me to do something extraordinary with my life."

What are your day-to-day coping skills?

I lived a life of abundance in a negative way. I let my parents down for a long time. They're not young and I don't know how much longer I have with them. I thank God that nothing happened to my parents when I was doing my drugs. I don't know how I would've rebounded from that, them seeing me last at my lowest point in my life. They keep me in check. But I struggle every day in trying to live the 'right' way; trying not to give in to my demons. It's an internal struggle. I have an addictive personality. I just know if I get back into it I'm going to die. I'm happy I didn't die back then from my accident. There's so much I want to do. I've been high on so many different kinds of drugs; but the high that I had rolling across America every day, meeting new people and affecting and stirring something up in them, and motivating and inspiring them was the greatest high, the greatest feeling I ever had by a long shot. That is where I'm most comfortable and where I'm happiest. This is what I know I need to do because I'm good at reaching out and connecting with people and that is what I think about every day. I created a platform for myself that contains credibility, a great work ethic, determination, will and desire and I proved it. Nobody can ever question if I have the ambition or the focus to accomplish whatever I want. If I don't take advantage of that, I'm an idiot.

What advice can you offer people going through difficult situations?

You have to be OK with it. You have to understand it's not anything more than an unfortunate circumstance, unless you created it yourself. You have to be able to work towards something; something that is meaningful, that makes your heart beat a little bit faster, makes your palms sweat, that excites you. You need that in your life. If you don't have that it's just a matter of time before you fall into a rut. Focus on something that you love. You have to be OK with yourself. I'm a forty-two-year-old man. I'm dating a woman. She gets upset when I don't want to sleep over at her house. I have no control over my bladder. That's my reality. I have to be OK with saying that. Once you're OK with the hand you've been dealt, as bad as it is, then everything is fair game. Then you can do anything you want. But if you're not OK with yourself, then you're going to have problems. You end up closing doors, limiting yourself and alienating people.

What is your purpose in doing these 'rolls'?

My purpose is to effect people in a way that makes them question where they're at in their life; to stir something up in people. There are so many people who have the desire to do something big. I think the uncertainty of it is why most don't shoot for it. They're afraid.

꙾

DO WE HAVE A 'PERSONHOOD' BEYOND OUR LIMITATIONS? The answer is unequivocally yes, as we have seen by these interviewees. It's hard to see though when we're in the midst of horrific, tragic circumstances. However, with time and hard emotional work around loss and grief, we grow in acceptance and we evolve into a new version of ourselves. We realize newfound strengths and potential. The grief is no longer a paralyzing feeling. We start to see possibilities within our new reality and are no longer limited by our disability.

Resource:
http://www.rollwithme.org/
Soon to be a documentary.

EPILOGUE

For some people who have suffered great adversity, life appears to be over. Remaining stuck in their pain, becoming bitter and miserable have become a way of living with challenges and loss. My hope, however, is that these interviews have shown that regardless of circumstances, life can be lived well. It is possible to rebuild and turn pain to purpose, and ultimately reclaim a rich meaningful life. No matter what our innate predisposition and make-up is, we can cultivate and grow new response patterns and stronger resiliency muscles that can propel us to live better despite our challenges. It is within our power.

The human spirit is limitless and we have reservoirs of untapped potential. The inherent state of being alive is a state of flux; we can be the change within our own lives to make and re-make as the tides continuously turn — albeit with rough, raging, waters at times.

There truly is life beyond our adverse circumstances. Purpose, attitude, faith and support are some of the main factors that can carry us through.

As Audrey Hepburn says, "Nothing is impossible; the word itself says "I'm possible!"

We are all possible!

You too can climb your personal mountain and begin to look out to a new horizon, a changed landscape, and create your new reality with renewed meaning and joy.

ABOUT THE AUTHOR

Harriet Cabelly

"Life is an occasion. Rise to it."

 As a social worker and positive psychology coach, Harriet's passion is working with people to help create their best possible life. She journeys with them as they cope and grow beyond their painful situations.

Harriet is an engaging speaker and workshop facilitator. She is a coaching expert on the WOR radio show, *Change Your Attitude, Change Your Life* and has appeared on ABC News as a parenting coach. She is a very fulfilled empty-nester — loving her work as well as time with her grandchildren, traveling and always looking to take on new adventures and learning opportunities.

This is her first book. She is thrilled to be getting the voices of these inspirational people out there so that everyone can benefit from their honesty and wisdom.